How to Be a **God Chaser** and a **Kid Chaser**

Prioritizing Passions While Parenting

Tommy and Thetus Tenney

Contributing authors:

Beth Alves

Stacey Campbell

Dr. James Dobson

Dr. Dick Eastman

Jane Hansen

Dr. Cindy Jacobs

Dutch and Ceci Sheets

T.F. Tenney

How to Be a God Chaser and a Kid Chaser

Fresh Bread

An Imprint of
Destiny Image® Publishers, Inc.
P.O. Box 310
Shippensburg, PA 17257-0310

ISBN 0-7684-5006-3
Library of Congress Catalog Card Number 2001 132712

For Worldwide Distribution
Printed in the U.S.A.

First Printing: 2001   Second Printing: 2001

This book and all other Destiny Image, Revival Press, MercyPlace, Fresh Bread, Destiny Image Fiction, and Treasure House books are available at Christian bookstores and distributors worldwide.

For a U.S. bookstore nearest you, call **1-800-722-6774**.
For more information on foreign distributors, call **717-532-3040**.
Or reach us on the Internet: **www.destinyimage.com**

Dedication

For me, the heritage of "God-chasing" began long before I was even born. Every morning about 9 o'clock, a little woman with a Bible tucked under her arm was closely observed by a young couple with kids and without God. My parents watched as this anonymous Christian walked past their apartment with a steady pace. She walked as though pursuing something...or someone. On her way to a daily prayer meeting this "God Chaser" influenced the course of the observant "kid chasers" in their apartment. I don't know the exact day destiny was determined for me, but I'm sure Heaven will not forget. The future will never be the same—not for me, nor for my children. An unknown influence had lit the flame of passion.

Thetus Tenney, his mom

My initial influences also entailed a small woman. Her pursuit began daily before I awoke. If I got up a bit early and ventured into the den or living room, I would see my mom "pursuing" in prayer—Bible open, heart panting, passionately chasing God! Quietly observing that daily discipline affected me. It remodeled the blueprint of my future—and perhaps left a small footprint in the sands of time to mark the passing of a "God Chaser."

Tommy Tenney, her son

Transparent in the struggles, triumphant in the Spirit—all eight of us will cheer you on as you run the dual race with kids, toward God. Encouragement can make a big difference. Empathy from those who've "been there" can be encouraging.

Their Friends

For all "kid chasers" with tired feet, but strong spirits,
For all "God Chasers" with sagging spirits
but soaring passions,
...this book is dedicated to you and yours.

Contents

Swinging my feet from the worn, well-used front pew of the little church in DeRidder, Louisiana, I was but the latest of a long line of boys who had helped rub the carpet threadbare in countless services. Watching as my mom sang the words of a long-since forgotten song:

"He washed my eyes with tears…
that I might see"

I wondered, at the age of five, "Whatever can she be crying about?"

Passion expressed is generationally contagious. Her passion for His presence ignited a flame in the heart of her small son. She probably doesn't remember that day…but I'll never forget it. I became what she had long been…a God Chaser. The chapters my mom wrote for this book have only reaffirmed my impressions as her five-year-old son.

Her son, Tommy.

Chapter 1

Am I a God Chaser or a Kid Chaser?

*...when I can't be in two places at one time,
I can be in two races.*

Thetus Tenney

I still remember the rainy day in late autumn. Our son, Tommy, would be three years old in February—and now we had our new baby girl, Teri. They were exactly what we had hoped for, a boy and a girl.

We actually chose their names on our honeymoon, and I wrote them on a napkin right under my new name, "Mrs. Tom Fred Tenney." Tom, Thetus, Tommy and Teri; that was what we wanted, hoped for, and prayed for. The thrill of expectancy had now become sweet reality. The seemingly carefree days of "just the two of us" had been replaced with the responsibility of "the four of us."

I remember that cool day when I was "twenty-something." I stared out of a window, blinking away the emotional rain of my tears while I watched the windshield wipers throw aside raindrops on our car as my husband drove away to his ministry

1

appointment. I was happy with the children and had vowed to myself that I would be the best mother I could possibly be. Yet, I had deep yearnings and the inward "stirring" of spiritual giftings—and a strong natural drive to be used of God.

I wanted to be involved in His Kingdom enterprise, but there I stood feeling left out and confused. I loved God and I loved my children, so what was I supposed to do? I wanted to do something for God—something significant. I had an overwhelming desire to be a God Chaser, but at the time I was overwhelmed with the responsibility of being a kid chaser.

I struggled with two callings: sainthood—chasing God, and parenthood—chasing kids; ministry and marriage.[1] I had two tracks: heavenly passion and earthly parenting; parallel pursuits. Both of them required time and energy, punctuated by continuous choices and decisions. Neither of them could ever really be completed in the space of time.

In a very simplistic way, I made a decision on that rainy day many years ago that has helped me balance spiritual pursuit and earthly responsibility. It helped keep me on track in my chase after God while chasing my lively children.

Perhaps it was more of a desperate decision than a well-thought-out, deliberate decision. I now know my frustration came from a heart desperately hungry after God. With two babies at home and a husband in a traveling ministry, I could either seethe in frustration or find a way to feed my spiritual hunger. I couldn't "do" too much at the time. It was all I could do just to "be" what I was, but I could prepare myself for the time when I would be able to do more.

I made my decision: I would read, study, pray and meditate in the precious few moments of a young mother's "down time" (at first, it was usually while the kids were down for their nap;

then later, when they were at school). I could also share with my growing children what has been one of my favorite lifelong pursuits of God—finding Him in nature. I did not realize then that the starting shot had been fired and I was off on a dual track race.

The Christian life is a marathon race, not a hundred-meter dash. It is a long haul over hills, through valleys, sweating it out in the heat, refreshed by a breeze, weary yet pursuing. Every mile marker can make a difference in the end result.

Little did I know then that decades later I would still be energized by that early decision of how I would chase God while chasing kids.

For a special seven years I carefully planned my time so that most evenings and every early morning would take me a little farther in my pursuit of God. I am by nature an early riser, and this was a time that suited my God-chasing efforts.

My Bible and my books fed my hunger for learning about Him. My prayers brought Him intimately near so that in meditation I learned from Him. The deliberate pursuit provided time to get to know Him.

Two tracks, parallel pursuits: chasing God and chasing kids. Is it an earthly race with a heavenly mind-set, or a heavenly race with an earthly mind-set? Perhaps we should say that chasing God while chasing kids is an earthly race with an eternal destiny!

Parenting and pursuing God are parallel pursuits with an eternal goal. If you are a passionate pursuer of God, then you have more likelihood of passing on your "spiritual DNA" to your children—a "genetic" predisposition to spiritual athletic prowess in pursuing Him. Much as a star athlete may pass

3

along the genes of a champion to his or her children, we have the very real possibility of passing along the eternal fervor of spiritual pursuit.

Some parents think nothing of their children seeing them return breathlessly to the house after an early morning jog in pursuit of good health. We should be even more willing to allow our children to see us in our passionate pursuit of the King of glory in early morning or afternoon prayer and devotion each day. It may well be the foundation for their priceless spiritual legacy as passionate God chasers.

Take a deep breath, and run!

About Thetus Tenney

Thetus Tenney has been in ministry for over 50 years. With her husband, Tom Fred, they have traveled internationally in various meetings, conferences, and seminars. She has assembled numerous large conferences for women, special leadership training and summons to prayer. Married for more than 40 years, they are blessed with a son and daughter, Tommy and Teri, who are both in ministry. They also enjoy their five wonderful grandchildren.

For further information about Thetus Tenney and her ministry, please contact:

Mrs. Thetus Tenney
Focused Light
P.O. Box 55
Tioga, LA 71477
Phone: 1-888-433-3355
E-mail: ThetusTenney@aol.com

Endnotes

1. Except where specific personal titles are used in conjunction with a name (e.g., St. Theresa), I am not using the words "sainthood" and "saints" to refer to individuals designated by various church bodies as worthy of special status or veneration due to extraordinary accomplishments. I am referring to every believer's "high calling in Christ" to be His disciples, to be ordinary worshipers who are continually being conformed to His image as we seek His face and do His will (see Rom. 1:7; 1 Cor. 1:2; Phil. 3:14; and Rom. 8:29).

Since his childhood, the hand of God has been evident on Tommy. His pursuit of God has fueled the flame of anointing that has taken him around the world to encourage other God chasers. He is no less passionate in his love for his wife, Jeannie, and their daughters.

His mom, Thetus Tenney.

Chapter 2

Prioritizing Your Passions

...when spiritual passion and parenting collide.

Tommy Tenney

At the end of the race, have we imparted to our children something that will last? Will we leave them an endless list of rules and regulations, or will we impart a legacy of passion for God and for one another?

Most of us remember one particular Bible character to this day simply because, in Jesus' words, she had "chosen the best portion."[1] What choices will frame your children's memories of you decades from now?

Have we chosen the "best portion" as parents struggling to chase God and somehow catch up with our children at the same time? Are we teaching them as much about the joy of His presence as about the proper place for dirty clothes, toys, and a civil tongue? I'm concerned that many Christian parents are modeling "spectator Christianity" rather than "God chaser passion." God clearly prefers "doers" over mere "hearers."[2] As I mentioned in my book, *God's Favorite House*, "Those who 'watch' without pursuing God themselves become mere spiritual 'voyeurs' whose lives lack the genuine relationship God desires for them."[3] Perhaps the greatest damage is done in the hearts of the children watching our spiritual charade.

There is heavenly truth in the earthy old axiom, "Actions speak louder than words." Whether you like it or not, your children will remember what you *do* better than what you *say*. Do you model the mercy, grace, and patience of God in front of them? Your example literally helps to shape your child's understanding of God and the proper priorities for life, marriage, and parenting.

We must prioritize two vital points of passion as Christian parents with children: First, our passion for God and His presence; and second, our passion for one another as married partners in life and parenthood. Both "passion points" invoke the picture of a bride and groom preserving their first love. As members of the Bride of Christ, we must pursue Him with the same passion and ardor revealed in the Song of Solomon. After all, He must be our First Love—not merely our part-time paramour.[4]

Passion Is Not a Dirty Word

One of the most important things you can do is "prioritize your passion" while parenting your children. Contrary to the myth that plagues many church circles, *passion* is not a dirty word. According to John in the Book of Revelation, the state of being "lukewarm" (we call it *apathy* today) is the real "dirty word" God hates with a "passion."[5]

As covenant partners, we must pursue our spouses and prioritize our passion for them. This is God's way of providing security, stability, and an *enduring legacy* for our children. Take time *for* one another so you won't end up taking things *from* one another.

One time early in our marriage, my wife and I really needed a break. I told her, "Honey, we need to take a few days off—just you and me." She told me, "Tommy, the kids are little and we really don't have the money to do that right now." I understood what she was saying and I knew she was right about our finances, but something far more important was at stake. I said, "Sweetheart, if we don't prioritize *our* relationship, then the whole framework for our children can fall apart."

Children are "products" of our marriage relationships. I am referring to more than the procreation process; I'm talking about the progressive process of building loving relationships that endure the test of time. While we make every effort to prioritize our passion for God and our spouses, we must also parent our children. Sometimes we make the parenting process too complex and difficult. Simplify the task by understanding the value of *everyday experiences* with your children.

"Drive-Through" Parenting Doesn't Work

Many North American parents operate by the "drive-up window" philosophy of parenting—they are in such a hurry to "get them grown and out the door" that they fail to enjoy their fleeting moments with their children. We should take our cue from Jesus. He did not view children as distractions, hindrances, or obstacles to His ministry or "career." Instead, He made them the centerpiece of some of His most important teachings on the Kingdom of Heaven! *"Let the little children come to Me...unless you are converted and become as little children, you will by no means enter the kingdom of heaven...."*[6]

God blessed me with the opportunity to write some well-received books about pursuing God's presence, but I am quick to admit that many of the most important things I've learned about "chasing God" and "catching God" were learned through experiences with my daughters.

He revealed to me why He sometimes "hides" from His children during one of my countless games of "hide and seek" with one of my daughters. He hides not so that He *cannot* be found, but so that He *can* be found.[7] He treasures those moments of joyous discovery and reunion that come when we finally "find" Him, because they lead to times of renewed intimacy and communion with us.

When my children were younger, I always looked forward to leaving the rigors of a busy day behind under the flood of exuberant hugs and kisses delivered by my three precious daughters. (They're all a bit older now, but they still brighten my days with their affectionate hugs, loving smiles, and sweet kisses.)

God used those common parenting experiences to reveal how important it was for me to seek His face more than the blessings of His hands. When I would return home from a ministry trip, my girls would often ask me if I brought back any gifts for them. I love to give my daughters gifts, but I really looked forward to the times my little girls would snuggle close enough to look me in the eyes and say, "I love you, Daddy." My girls temporarily forgot all their questions about gifts while in the lap and arms of the "giver."

As I wrote in *The God Chasers*, "Father God wishes for the same thing. God chasers want God! Not even the 'things of God' will satisfy someone who is a 'man after God's own heart' (see Acts 13:22)."[8] He treasures those moments when we seek Him for His own sake rather than for what He can do for us; when we seek His face, not just His hands.

Above All—Model Unconditional Love

I made it a point to train my daughters about the unconditional love their mother and I have for them. As I explained in my book, *God's Dream Team*, hardly two days would go by without me asking my girls, "What are you supposed to always remember?" The answer was always the same: "My Daddy loves me." Then I would expand the lesson: "When does he love you?" They would answer, "All the time." I'd ask, "Does he love you when you are good?" When they answered yes, I'd ask them, "Does he love you when you are bad?" The answer was always yes. In this way, I also established an unyielding truth in their hearts about the unconditional love of their heavenly Father.[9]

Every time you hold your children and allow their painful playground problems to fade in the security of your arms, you impart a lasting imprint that will lead them to the comfort of God's everlasting arms in their adult years. In those nurturing moments with your children, remember the comfort *you* find in God's presence, and in the arms of your spouse in times of stress or difficulty. Take that golden opportunity to thank Him for His blessings once again.

David, prioritizing his passion for God with his love for his family, dealt with the pain of losing his infant borne by Bathsheba. He knew the unique pain felt by a father whose daughter has been raped. In fact, King David was forced to banish his eldest son, Absalom, after he rashly murdered the man who ravished Tamar, his sister. Things went from bad to worse when Absalom rebelled against his own father, usurped the throne of Israel, ravished David's concubines, and even tried to kill his own father.

Yet, David was known as a worshiper; even though he was also a terribly human parent whose home was wracked by the fruits of his parental favoritism, political intrigue, and all of the tangled problems experienced in "blended marriages" (he had many wives).

I understand what it means to "parent through the pain." I have had to worship my way through some of the situations David experienced—trying to prioritize passions for both God and family. If the situation is the same—the answer is always the same: *When it hurts, keep loving.*

The Show Goes On in Private and in Public

Remember that life does not take place in a vacuum—it occurs on the open stage of the family. One of the best-known phrases from the entertainment industry is, "The show must go on." Where your family is concerned, the "show" goes on in public and in private because your children see you in both realms. This offers you a tremendous opportunity to demonstrate the kind of genuine Christianity that spans the full range of human experience—including the good and the bad.

My parents have been wonderful role models for me. For instance, they never fought in front of me. As I noted in *God's Dream Team*, "I understand that there were some words said, but the exchanges never happened in front of me or my sister. I am the product of a family filled with unity. What that gives to children is of immeasurable value."[10]

They also did a good job of "being normal while being supernatural" at the same time. I remember attending white-hot revival meetings as a child. But just as vividly, I also remember hilarious family times playing games while camping out in the Smokey Mountains.

How do you do it? Establish your priorities and stake out time and opportunities to pursue those priorities. Prioritize your pursuit of God by shutting yourself away in the proverbial (or literal) "prayer closet" for times of intimate worship, prayer, intercession, and study of His Word. (In some seasons of parenthood, you may need to make do with short segments of worship or study time sandwiched in with daily duties.)

Just as parents sometimes lock their bedroom door to preserve the priority of periods of uninterrupted communication and marital intimacy, so must we sometimes "close our door" on the outside world for vital times of uninterrupted communication and family intimacy.

Every action we take to prioritize passion in personal worship, the marriage relationship, and quality family time becomes a living lesson to our children about prioritizing passion in their own lives. Passionate parents in continued pursuit of their spouses can produce passionate marriages in their children's lives. Passionate parents in pursuit of God can produce passionate children in God's kingdom. Heavenly passion and earthly parenting can mix!

About Tommy Tenney

Tommy Tenney is the author of the best-selling books *The God Chasers*, *God's Dream Team*, *God's Favorite House*, and *The God Catchers*. He pastored for almost ten years and has spent nearly two decades as an itinerant minister, sharing his passion for the presence of

God with countless churches in more than 40 nations. Tommy is a well-known revivalist who has been used to both spark and fuel the fires of revival. He has experienced the miraculous, but most importantly, he has rediscovered the secret power of intimacy with and humility before God. Tommy and his wife, Jeannie, reside in Louisiana with their three daughters. One gerbil, one hamster, a parakeet, and two Yorkies—Little Romeo and Nicholas—round out the Tenney household.

For further information about Tommy Tenney and his ministry, please contact:

Tommy Tenney
GodChasers.Network
P.O. Box 3355
Pineville, LA 71361
www.godchasers.net

Endnotes

1. Mary, the sister of Martha and Lazarus, was praised for "choosing the best portion" after her older sister asked Jesus to correct Mary for sitting at His feet instead of leaving the room to help Martha in the kitchen. Jesus unexpectedly praised Mary for choosing "the best portion" while explaining His action to Martha (see Lk. 10:38-42). The balance required in this dynamic tension and interaction of ministries is the subject of my new book, *Chasing God, Serving Man* (Shippensburg, PA: Fresh Bread, an imprint of Destiny Image Publishers, 2001).

2. See Jas. 1:22.

3. *God's Favorite House* (Shippensburg, PA: Fresh Bread, an imprint of Destiny Image Publishers, 1999), p. 91.

4. See Rev. 2:4.

5. See Rev. 3:16.

6. Mk. 10:14b and Mt. 18:3b, respectively.

7. This simple story is the core truth upon which I based the sequel to *The God Chasers*; a book entitled *The God Catchers* (Nashville, TN: Thomas Nelson Publishers, 2000).

8. Tommy Tenney, *The God Chasers* (Shippensburg, PA: Destiny Image Publishers, 1998), p. 54.

9. Adapted from a personal anecdote I included in my book *God's Dream Team: A Call to Unity* (Ventura, CA: Regal Books, 1999), p. 82.

10. Ibid, p. 81.

Jane Hansen is known internationally for her work as President and CEO of Aglow International. We know her as a dear friend with whom we've shared many life experiences. She is loved around the world for her endearing quality of transparent honesty, along with her gifts, talents, and total commitment to God.

Tommy and Thetus Tenney

Chapter 3

They May Run Faster Than You—But They Can't Run Faster Than God

...when your dreams turn into nightmares.

Jane Hansen

Chasing God while chasing kids often doesn't stop when the children get old enough to be out from under our feet. Sometimes the chase on both levels intensifies. Listen to Jane Hansen's story as she tells of her pursuit of God for a wayward child, which resulted in much more than the return of a prodigal. It produced a critical change in her own heart that has helped shape the message she brings to men and women all over the world.

The clock struck midnight. 1:00 a.m. 2:00 a.m. 3:00 a.m. Still no sign of Jeff. Where could he be at this hour? Even in asking the question, my heart already knew the answer. This scene had been played out more times than I cared to remember in the last several years. Usually, just before dawn, he would stagger through the door, drunk or high on drugs, or both.

Jeff's terrifying downward spiral started in junior high when he became involved with the wrong crowd. By eleventh grade, he had dropped out of school, left home and had immersed himself in a motorcycle gang. His living conditions grew more and more grim as the drugs and alcohol increasingly crippled his judgment and ability to hold a job.

I can't tell you the incredible pain I experienced during that period of my life. I was a Christian, I cried out to God, yet all I had hoped and believed for my son's life was slipping out of reach. I tried to talk with my husband, but it was a difficult time in our marriage. We weren't able to connect in a way that would have given me the strength and support I needed.

The stress we were experiencing with Jeff only exacerbated the alienation between us. We couldn't even talk about Jeff's situation, much less pray about it together. His solution was denial, anger, and more rules. Jeff just needed more good, old-fashioned discipline, he said. I was sick with worry and heart-broken with grief over what was occurring in my family. Chaos and tension permeated our home, affecting our two younger children as well.

My Dreams Were Disintegrating Before My Eyes

The dreams I had cherished for my life—a loving husband, wonderful children, a home I could call my own and decorate to my heart's content—were all disintegrating before my eyes. Something had gone terribly wrong and try as I might, I couldn't fix it. Every area of my life seemed broken beyond hope. Yet God used this excruciatingly painful time in my life to do a deep work in my heart that ultimately affected far more than my son's deliverance.

One day, as I was ironing, the Lord spoke gently to my heart, "It is my desire to restore. Not primarily for your sake, but for Mine. You will reap the overflow." Then, slowly and persistently, over the next several months, the Lord began to turn my focus—from me to *Him*. I discovered that many of my prayers through the years had been more about wanting to find happiness and fulfillment in my relationship with my husband, my children and in my home, than they were about God's purposes. I realized I had been looking to my family for life instead of turning to God as my source. As God uncovered my heart, I began to see beyond my unfulfilled desires and longings to understand God's desires for me, my husband, and our children.

As I pressed into God for answers, through prayer and His Word, a new understanding of my purpose and significance as a woman began to emerge. Proverbs 31 brought new revelations about what it means to be a "virtuous woman." I discovered that "virtuous" in the Hebrew (*chayil*) is a dynamite word. More than moral and chaste, it actually means "strong and able." The virtuous woman is one of might and power, a woman who is "war worthy." Someone who is war worthy is ready to go to war and has one thought in mind: to win. I became aware that I was involved in a war for my son's life and there came a resolve in my heart that I would do everything in my power to win! The virtuous woman is a warrior woman!

The root of *chayil* means "to labor, to travail and bring forth life." As women, we instinctively know how to bring forth life in the natural realm. It's the way God made us. But He was teaching me a deeper truth: just as He created us to bring forth life in the physical, so had He placed within us the capacity to travail and bring to birth things in the spiritual realm. As we allow God to turn our hearts from our self-center to Him, He will begin to use the very nature He placed within us to birth His purposes in our families, our churches, our communities, and even our nations.

Some Days I Would Prostrate Myself on the Floor

As I was being turned from myself, my heart began to pulsate with the desire to see our home restored for God's sake, just as He had spoken to me. Spiritually I began to feel like a woman "great with child." A spirit of intercession, totally uninitiated by me and unlike anything I had experienced before, settled upon me.

At the time, I knew little about intercession. What I did know was that this child of mine was headed for destruction and the weight and grief of the situation led me to cry out to God. There were days when I would prostrate myself on the floor, my only prayers being unintelligible groans and travail, weeping before God. At other times, as I was going about my daily routine, I would sense a heaviness, a knowing that I needed to pray. I found myself letting God use my mouth to speak into being what was on His heart, to call forth those "things that are not as though they were."[1]

My understanding of spiritual warfare grew. Two passages in Proverbs 31 stood out to me: "She seeks wool and flax, and willingly works with her hands. She is not afraid of snow...for all her household is clothed with scarlet [symbolic of the blood of Jesus shed for our sins]."[2] In Scripture, snow and "cold" are sometimes representative of God's judgment against sin. The term *wool*, *like scarlet*, can signify a covering from judgment.[3] Flax, the raw material used to make linen, represents righteousness.

I Cooperated With God's Spirit of Intercession

The virtuous woman works willingly with her hands to ensure that her family will be covered in God's righteousness in the blood of Christ, so they will be protected from ultimate judgment. Two different Hebrew words are used to describe "hands" in Proverbs 31. The word *kaph* refers to hands extended to God in intercession, beseeching Him on behalf of another. The word *yad* refers to warring hands that fight to win the victory. Psalm 144:1 declares, "the Lord...trains my hands [*yad*] for war, and my fingers for battle."

As I cooperated with God's spirit of intercession, I knew my "hands" were warring against the spiritual darkness that was destroying Jeff's life. I remember one day in particular. In my prayer closet (which was literally a closet!), I announced to the enemy that he had gone this far and could go no farther in the Hansen household. I declared, "In the name of Jesus I push back the forces of darkness and I call forth light!"

To seal that proclamation, I went to my front door and to every other door post in the house and anointed each of them with oil in faith, claiming God's promises for my family. Where Jeff was concerned, I prayed, "Lord, I release him to You. I don't just want a young man who is cleaned up and off drugs. Do whatever You have to do to bring forth a man of God." That is a fearful prayer for a mother to pray, but *my confidence in God's ability to deliver my son was becoming greater than my son's inability to follow God!*

After this event I continued to pray and speak aloud the promises of God from His Word over Jeff's life. I did it in my prayer closet, while I worked around the house, and while driving in my car. I continually invited the Holy Spirit to have authority over our home.

Then one day, I knew the warfare had been accomplished. It was as though the spirit of intercession that had been upon me was lifted. I couldn't have worked up another prayer if I had tried. Nothing had changed in Jeff's life at that point, but I knew I had been obedient to the Lord. I waited...and I trusted.

God Delivered Him Completely

About six months later, Jeff experienced a complete turn-around in his life. He instantly turned away from drugs and alcohol. Cigarettes took a little longer, but God delivered him completely from every addiction that was destroying his life. Friends had always been very important to Jeff, but God changed that as well. For a season, he walked without any friends at all, choosing instead to rely upon God for strength to stand. His hunger for the Word of God grew as he gained tremendous insights from the Lord. Today, Jeff is a man of God who walks daily with the Lord.

God is concerned about *your* children too. They may be old enough to run faster than you can, but they can't run faster than God. If they are grown and out of your reach, then you need to chase God—He will chase your children and train *you* up for His Kingdom in the process!

About Jane Hansen

Jane Hansen has served as President and CEO of Aglow International since 1980. She has traveled extensively throughout the world noting the significance of women and encouraging them in their spiritual pursuits. Jane was married to her late husband, Howard, for more than forty years. They were blessed with three children, Jeff, Scott, and Lisa, who have added the blessing of eleven grandchildren.

For further information about Jane Hansen and her ministry, please contact:

Jane Hansen
Aglow International
P.O. Box 1749
Edmonds, WA 98020-1749
Ph: 425-775-7282
www.aglow.org

Endnotes

1. See Rom. 4:17 NIV.
2. Pr. 31:13,21.
3. See Ps. 147:16-17; Hos. 2:9.

Chapter Four

How to Be What I Can't Become

...when He says I'm a saint, but I feel like an "ain't."

Thetus Tenney

*A*t least one first-century God chaser, a man named Paul, perceived the pursuit of God as a race. It is obvious—he peppers his writings with key words and phrases such as *runners*, *gets the prize*, *competes*, *training*, *run* [the race] *with perseverance*, and more.[1]

One particular passage in his letter to the church at Philippi has always intrigued me, despite its complex construction. (Sometimes I wish Paul had taken a course in concise writing!) He wrote:

> *Not that I have already attained, or am already perfected; but I press on, that I may lay hold of that for which Christ Jesus has also laid hold of me. Brethren, I do not count myself to have apprehended; but one thing I do, forgetting those things which are behind and reaching forward to those things which are ahead,*

I press toward the goal for the prize of the upward call of God in Christ Jesus.[2]

Certain things in this passage especially speak to me about "the race on two tracks"—the parallel pursuit of God and your children. First, I was drawn to the place where Paul said in essence, "Not that I have already been made perfect..." What a relief! I don't have to despair because I'm not perfect. (This is an honest admission!) The truth is that I never will be satisfied until I awake in His likeness.[3] I'm thankful that God sees us as an ongoing, ever-growing work, and as long as we are on track, reaching, striving, and pressing, we are "perfect" in process. This is also true concerning our pursuit of parenthood and sainthood. I became a parent because I have children, but becoming a parent does not mean I became a perfect parent. I became a "saint" by the grace of God, but all the while I'm still an "ain't"! I "ain't" perfect! I am still in process!

I am not sure where I first heard it, but someone has said, "There are those who are all flesh with no Spirit, but there are none of us who are all Spirit with no flesh." How true! The greatest and the best among us must still contend with fleshly imperfections. Even our Bible heroes wore tilted halos and tracked through life with feet of clay! The Bible is a "tell all" book—it boldly reveals the good, the bad, the brave, the fearful, the strong, and the weak in its unrelenting honesty.

- Moses "the meek" was so incited by the continuous complaining of the Israelites that he lost his temper. "You rebels," he shouted, and hit the rock to bring forth water rather than speak to it as God had said.[4]

- Jacob became the possessor of the birthright as a manipulating conniver. With his mother's help, he tricked his old, blind father into thinking he was his twin brother, Esau. He really stole what was to have been Esau's.[5]

- Righteous Lot considered compromising his family. He offered to give his two virgin daughters to the wild and perverted men of Sodom.[6]

These and so many more were not the perfectly painted stained-glass saints we often believe they were. They are "bone of our bone, flesh of our flesh." All of us are cut from the same bolt of the cloth called "humanness." Even the intense apostle Paul readily admitted to battling with the daily contention of flesh and Spirit. He said, "When I want to do good, I don't. And when I try not to do wrong, I do it anyway."[7]

The difference between the saints and the "aint's" is their commitment to "becoming." We must let the miles and the trials, the years and the tears, and our victories and defeats mold us and make us more like Him—in spite of ourselves.

Many of us seem to stumble over our own clumsiness while pursuing perfect sainthood and parenthood. I'm thankful our heavenly Father "...has compassion on His children...for He knows how we are formed, He remembers that we are dust."[8] His compassion as an understanding and merciful Father to us allows us to stay on track in the dual race of parenthood and sainthood. I keep on growing up in Christ, and I want to be just like my heavenly Father.

Alan Redpath once said, "The conversion of a soul is the miracle of a moment. The manufacture of a saint is the task of a lifetime."[9] Spiritual perfection is in the "pressing on" part of life. Dr. Richard Dobbins also helped to ease my fears concerning perfected parenting when I heard him say, "The average child can withstand the average mistakes of the average parent."

While we struggle with these parallel pursuits—chasing God while chasing kids—we must remember that both pursuits are "always in the making" and each teaches us about the other.

Tom Barnes, the dear old prophet-mentor in my life, once told me a story I have never forgotten. He had been having a lot of difficulty with someone in his church whom he sincerely felt was wrong. Much harm and hurt had resulted from what had been done. He decided that "enough was enough," and he went to his study fully intending to commit this rebel to God for severe chastisement. He knelt and began to tell God what he thought this rebel deserved and how he intended to deal with him, but God whispered: "Tom, you pray for him the way you would if he was your child."

This lesson taught became a lesson learned. Every parent is but a child (of God); and every child is a parent and a saint in the making. Since there are no trial runs for parenthood or sainthood, the chase needs grace for both the pursued and the pursuer.

One situation I encountered in my maturing years has provided me grace and hope to cope with my many mistakes and inadequacies as a parent. I always used to view my parents as wonderfully close to perfection. As I matured, I began to realize that they really were human with various strengths and weaknesses. This endeared them more to me as I observed them pressing on to become greater and more than what their humble beginnings could have ever predicted. It also gave me hope for myself. My own striving in the chase after God and kids has been strengthened by the humanness and divine aspirations of my parents.

The second key phrase in Paul's statement is, "I press on, that I may lay hold of that for which Christ Jesus has also laid hold of me."[10] What is this? Chasing and catching...does that mean "being chased and being caught"? Absolutely! As I pursue God, the pleasure of momentarily catching His presence produces the spiritual energy to run again. It is never a conclusive goal. Thankfully, my children caught this concept. As my son, Tommy, says, "God chasers have known this. They were willing to chase the 'uncatchable,' knowing the 'impossible' would catch them."[11]

I pursue God for my sufficiency. Then God pursues me for His destiny. And so it is with our children.

With the birth of a child, the race is on—as anyone can tell you who has ever shared a house with a two-year-old or a pre-driving teen. You can run constantly, day after day, but you never seem to catch up with all the cries, requests, and endless duties. Then those you chased finally streak onward, and the pursued becomes the pursuer.

Living between the tension of parenting responsibilities and spiritual aspirations can often leave you unsure if you are doing either as well as you wish. The clutter of life, the clash of wills, busy schedules, the weight of worry, the trying to become and the hope and prayers that in the midst of all this the God part, the God destiny, will impact and emerge in your children. This is every godly parent's supreme success symbol.

There are many stories I could tell about my own son and daughter, but among the vivid memories I hold dear are the first times I heard each of them speak, as young adults, to an audience of which I was a part. Their messages were good, well prepared and well delivered, but more importantly their God-hunger was evidenced by their passion. I was truly humbly proud! While proud of their ability, I was also humbled by the fact that in spite of my own human imperfections, they had caught the passion of their parents in pursuing God.

If this blessing from your children has not yet been yours, let me share another story.

The old pastor had been faithful. Impeccable character, righteousness, and justice were his marks. Strong prayers and notable miracles accompanied his ministry. But he suffered a severe heartache—a wayward child. Devastating discouragement drove him to his knees. "Lord, You just don't understand. You never had a wayward child." Then a bold but warm Presence of words filled his depressed mind. "Son, I have you." Recollected memories of the grace of God during his wayward years replaced his discouragement with hope. Like Gideon, after his exhausting victory over the armies of Midian, he had grown faint but was still pursuing.[12] The years rolled on, the chase continued—for both God and his daughter. He has not yet reached the end of his race for God, but his daughter made the turn and joined him in the race to see God's face.

An old farmer once gave me some words of wisdom. I was teaching a weekday Bible class made up mostly of women and a few retired men. He was a loving, but crusty old fellow who had not served God all of his life. My subject that day concerned sowing in righteousness. Someone brought up the negative aspect of "what you sow, you will also reap." The dear old farmer narrowed his eyes and spoke: "Well, I guess you can rotate the crops and change the harvest." So if, as a parent, your fear for your child's future springs from your past, get busy! Sow seeds of righteousness and change the harvest.

Paul's "attaining the unattainable" and "lay[ing] hold of that for which Christ Jesus has also laid hold of me" included a good dose of "forgetting those things which are behind."[13] Stretching and pressing, he knew the goal was in the going. So, if you have had weak knees in your chase after God and your kids—forget what you haven't done, do your best at what you know to do, get up and get going. Your strength for the chase can be perfected in your weakness.[14] His grace is sufficient for His child—and for your child.

In the yard of the house where we lived as Tommy and Teri were growing up were several very large, tall trees. These were wonderful play areas, providing not only much needed shade from the hot Louisiana summer sun, but inviting all kinds of fun play times.

In the front yard was a large magnolia tree. No grass grew under it and the big shiny green leaves made a lush, inviting canopy. Big limbs extended horizontally so near the ground it was a wonderful invitation for climbing. Even better, they were spaced just right for young feet and legs to ascend to dangerous heights very easily.

From a parent's view, we knew that those wonderfully spaced, big sturdy limbs could also make a fall from very high up a tragic accident; so we set strict limits on how high they could climb. One day, Tommy's dad came home at an unexpected time. Getting out of the car, he saw Tommy perched high up in the magnolia tree. He calmly walked over and watched as Tommy carefully descended, and they came into the house together.

Tom went to his study for pen and paper, then he wrote, "If I do not respect my father and his authority, I will not respect the authority of the policeman, my school teacher and eventually God Himself." Then he explained to a wide-eyed, disobedient little boy why respect and authority were important and the dangerous consequences of disobedience. Finally, he sent Tommy to his room to memorize what he had written. From time to time, as he grew up, his father asked him to quote it...and to this day, he still can.

Sociologists call this "patterning-training" for an expected, long-term outcome. As Tommy got a little older, I allowed him to sit with his friends at church (a safe distance from me). We established a little signal—when I saw him talking or misbehaving, I would clear my throat and immediately he would look at me and get the unspoken message.

Many years later, Tommy and Jeannie came to preach at our church. He was sitting on the platform next to his father. I was on the second row in front of them. With a giggle in my memory, I wondered what would happen if I cleared my throat. I did. Immediately our eyes locked and each of us had to smother a private laugh.

There is training for the chase. "Everyone who competes...goes into strict training."[15] God's Word also says, "Train a child in the way he should go and when he is old he will not turn from it."[16] And finally, in the words of the prophet Isaiah: "Learn to do right...."[17] Learning is the process of practice.

In the back yard of that house long ago, there were very tall pine trees. On one Sunday afternoon, as I started up the stairs for an afternoon nap, I looked out the window just in time to see that the children (there were several extras in the yard) had pulled the rope swing that hung from a limb of one of the pine trees over to the little playhouse. They were standing on top of the playhouse and taking turns jumping off while holding on to the rope. It did look like quite a fun and exciting feat, but the cautious terror rose up from the mother in me.

I very foolishly shouted to Teri who was the next one to swing, "You had better be careful! You could fall and break your arm, and if you do I'll spank you all the way to the hospital!" (Shame on me! I told you I wasn't perfect!) I had hardly stretched out on the bed before I heard a terrifying scream. Immediately I knew what had happened—and so it was.

My precious little girl, helped by her brother, was running toward the back door with a most terribly twisted broken arm. I cried with her (but did not spank her) all the way to the hospital. She tells me she was afraid I would really spank her, but she didn't understand how much I loved her.

So God is with us, His children. He warns us, and we foolishly proceed to get in trouble. Fearfully we bring our twisted mistakes to Him only to find that our weakness evokes the strength of His love. With God's help, we can attain the unattainable. As Tommy says, "God isn't interested in meeting you at your best—*that is really when you are at your worst*. He isn't interested in blessing your independence; He responds to your dependence. His strength is attracted to your weakness. He casts down the proud, but He runs to the pitiful."[18]

Endnotes

1. See 1 Cor. 9:24-26; Heb. 12:1.
2. Phil. 3:12-14.
3. See Ps. 17:15.
4. See Num. 20:10-12.
5. See Gen. 27.
6. See Gen. 19:8.
7. Rom. 7:19, *New Living Translation.*
8. Ps. 103:13-14 NIV.
9. Alan Redpath, *The Making of a Man of God* (Old Tappan, NJ: Fleming H. Revell, 1962), p. 5.
10. Phil. 3:12b
11. Tommy Tenney, *The God Catchers* (Nashville, TN: Thomas Nelson Publishers, 2000), p. 151.
12. See Judg. 8:4.
13. See Phil. 3:13-14.
14. See 2 Cor. 12:9.
15. 1 Cor. 9:25 NIV.
16. Pr. 22:6 NIV.
17. Is. 1:17 NIV.
18. Tommy Tenney, *The God Catchers* (Nashville, TN: Thomas Nelson Publishers, 2001), p. 100. (See also Psalm 101:5; Judges 2:18.)

Wesley and Stacey Campbell are a vivacious young couple with an infectious spirit. Stacey's dedication sustains her in the midst of a hectic life. Her solutions to balancing parental duty with spiritual desire are practical, and practicality is necessary if you hope to cope with five children and a strenuous travel schedule. Her frustrations haven't dampened her fervency.

Tommy and Thetus Tenney

Chapter 5

Married, With Children

...when duty and desire disagree.

Wesley & Stacey Campbell

(written from Stacey's perspective)

I fell in love with the Person of God by praying the Scriptures. The more I prayed, the more I loved Him. As these longings grew, I felt I would do anything and everything for Him. I often read books about great people who did awesome things for God and of others who spoke of constantly living in His presence. As I read these accounts, I fluctuated between frustration with my own life and a burning passion to do *anything* for Him. I was searching for more of God, and I wanted to know how I could best pursue Him.

As I grew in the Lord, I discovered the devotional mystics—those prophetic luminaries who would spend hours in prayer "gazing on Jesus," and then come down from their mystical mountains with the word of the Lord. I was in awe of people like Mary of Bethany and the apostle John in the Bible. Later, I discovered the writings of saints like St. Teresa of Avila, Teresa of Lisieux, and Mother Teresa of Calcutta. The insights I gleaned from their writings stayed with me in my spirit every day.

What shocked me about these saints was their prayer life. The intimidating information told me they all prayed every day—sometimes for many hours each day. It was from this secret place of prayer that their lives grew to impact the Kingdom.

As one book led to another, I found that since the early days of the Church in Jerusalem, there has been a "wrestling match" between the contemplative life (epitomized in the ascetic lives of the Desert Fathers), and the active life (epitomized by the preaching and mercy-oriented Orders of the Church).

Silence, Solitude, and Kids Usually Don't Mix

There was only one problem for me, though. I noticed that almost all of my "heroes and heroines" were *single*, *celibate*, and *contemplative*. That is, they liked silence and solitude. My problem was, of course, that I was married and not celibate. In my case, any contemplative silence I might hope for was promptly shattered by five small children (four of whom were *boys!*), and by a husband who is the consummate activist. For

Wesley, if two children are good, then five are better! If one conference a year is good, then fifty conferences is fifty times better. His favorite word is *more*!

When a spiritual renewal broke out in North America and Great Britain, cries of "More, Lord!" erupted everywhere and my husband felt the whole world was playing his song. His only problem was that his "dance partner" (me!) was pregnant with child number five, and child number one was only seven at the time! That wasn't exactly the best time, in my personal opinion, to embark on international preaching and prayer missions!

In spite of my circumstances in life, we began traveling all over the world within a matter of weeks—along with a newborn, a toddler, a pre-school child, a kindergartner, and a son in the second grade!

"God chasing" suddenly took on a whole new meaning. I went from praying in my bedroom and teaching two-year-olds in Sunday School to visiting fifty to seventy-five cities a year with a family of five children! We were "home" for only two months out of twelve each year.

We moved from one city to the next every three or four days, complete with five kids and thirty-five bags! I was also home schooling, and I ministered with my husband as many as three times a day. My newborn daughter accompanied me to six countries before she was even eight months old!

Although I knew this was part of God's plan for our family, it took me a while to catch up with this "suddenly season" of the Spirit. I had to really pray about the changes that were thrust upon us because I needed God's grace to embrace them. He revealed some things to me that may help you chase God while "married, with children."

Life B.C. (Before Children)

I found that life "B.C." was way different than life "A.C." (after children). "B.C.," I could keep up with my prayer life (and I could *almost* keep up with my husband). I prayed at home almost every day and I had a very close walk with the Lord.

Things were different "A.C." As each new baby came along, I had less time and less energy. I was often tired, and fatigue caused me to be easily irritated. My ideals of prayer and contemplation began to slip away in the daily reality of diapers, sleep deprivation, a messy house, and church obligations. (We also served as the senior pastoral couple of a growing thousand-member church where we led in a weekly prophetic prayer group, and I taught the two-year-olds in Sunday School).

As time went on, sermons about "doing great things for God" no longer inspired me; they depressed me. I couldn't even keep up with housework and laundry, let alone "do something great for God." Even the idea of doing "little things with great love" seemed out of reach. I felt tired and irritable, not loving! I spent more of my prayer time repenting than praising. I loved God, but "chasing Him" seemed like a far-off and exhausting dream. Instead, my life focused on chasing five active children in the middle of growing ministry commitments.

I asked the Lord to help me and He gave me some simple keys for overcoming. One key was the gift of praying in the Spirit. According to the Bible, the Holy Spirit helps us in our weakness by interceding for us "with groans that words cannot express."[1] When we pray in the Spirit, we "edify" or build up ourselves and our faith.[2] I learned that when my mind did not know what to say, the Spirit helped me express the inexpressible.

I just started praying in the Spirit every day, as often as I could. Over time, I grew stronger inside, and my prayer times became fruitful once again.

Seeking Silence in the Sanctuary of the Bathroom

How can we reconcile the contemplative life with the active life? One day I was so determined to find some silence that I locked myself in the bathroom (it was the only room in the house with a lock on it). It was the only way I could slip away to a private place to sit and think.

What does the Bible really say about it? I reasoned that God made man and woman to be fruitful and multiply. With this human "fruit" came mouths to feed, diapers to change, clothes to wash, and land to cultivate. This all took time...a great deal of time! For some, this season of life seems to take *all* of their time.

Surely God never intended to limit my desire to chase Him to the few hours I was in church or in prayer! Surely the bulk of my day was something I could offer Him as "a reasonable service."[3] My hunger for Him is too great to be contained in a single church service or the few moments when I can steal away with Him each day. I give Him what He gave me—my life and my body; even when it is driving here and there, picking up this and that, cooking, cleaning, nurturing, and just plain loving the people around me.

Perhaps it is true that by human reckoning, it might be more productive if I led a hundred people to Christ a day, or prayed for five hours a day. However, I was not celibate (only a microscopic number of Christians are called to that life anyway). My reproductive organs worked just fine, and a family was the result. So I am stuck with the question, "How can I chase Him while I chase my children?"

"It Is Enough for Me That You Die Daily."

Part of my answer came one day while I was praying and meditating on the Book of Revelation. I was in Revelation chapter 6 where it talks about the martyrs, and it had me thinking. I spent quite a bit of time praying about martyrdom that day, and then I heard the Lord say to me as clear as a bell, *"It is enough for Me that you die daily."* This simple phrase revealed to me that God takes as much pleasure in our small daily sacrifices as He does in one great act of service.

Another part of my answer came while reading a little book about a cook in a monastery whose name was "Brother Lawrence." Brother Lawrence also struggled with the question of what chasing God "looked like." What did God really want from Him?

At first, he thought the best way to chase God was to retire from society and live the solitary life of an ascetic. He found that this didn't work for him, and he experienced alternating feelings of joy and sadness, and peace and anxiety. Eventually, he felt God wanted him to become a lay brother of the Carmelite Order.

Brother Lawrence launched into an intense period of prayer, but his efforts to "push" into prayer only led him to another struggle with self-doubt and guilt over his own sinfulness and unworthiness. He spent ten years engulfed in intense anxiety during which he even began to doubt his own salvation. Brother Lawrence continued to pray until he finally cried out to God in desperation, "It no longer matters to me what I do or what I suffer, provided that I remain lovingly united to Your will."

The Continuous Practice of the Presence of God

God opened Brother Lawrence's eyes and he received a divine revelation of God's majesty that flooded his heart. As he meditated on the character and lovingkindness of God from that day on, his own character was changed. Brother Lawrence spent the next 40 years of his life in the "continuous practice of the presence of God," a process that he described as "a quiet, familiar conversation."

Brother Lawrence learned that his most effective way of communicating with God was to simply "practice His presence" while doing his "ordinary" work. He performed his work each day from a motive of love for God, and thought it was wrong to treat his prayer time differently from any other time. He felt that everything we do in the course of life should bring us into union with God, much as prayer brings us into communion with Him in our quiet times.

He advised those who desired God to seek Him in all of the activities of life and not to dichotomize between the spiritual and the mundane.[4] The Bible puts it this way: "And whatever you do in word or deed, do all in the name of the Lord Jesus, giving thanks to God the Father through Him."[5]

More and more, I've realized that God looks at the heart, not the action. A widow's mite is always worth more to Him than a Pharisee's riches. He will never forget the oil a prostitute pours on His feet, but He openly opposes the pride of the self-righteous. In time, I came to sense His peace just as strongly while wiping a runny nose at home as when I was speaking to thousands of people. I learned to sense His approval and joyful presence whether I was teaching two-year-olds or prophesying in major international ministry conferences. I sensed His presence as strongly while doing pastoral counseling as when I picked up the laundry—well, almost!

It is your motive, not your action, that God most cares about. Each of us has different callings and talents—our assignment is simply to be faithful in what He has given us. The heavenly Father does not love you or me for what we do; He loves us simply for who we are. I don't know about you, but I can't help but chase a Person who loves me with such unconditional love!

About Stacey Campbell

Stacey Campbell is the mother of five children. She began traveling and ministering internationally with her family when her children were all under eight years of age. She and her husband, Wesley, are the founding pastors of New Life Church in Kelowna, British Columbia, in Canada. They are directors of Hope for the Nations, an international mercy mission that specifically focuses on "children at risk." They also serve as directors of "Revival Now!" Ministries, and as producers of the "Praying the Bible" audiotape and CD series. Stacey is a teacher by profession, a prophetic person by gifting, and a lover of God by passion!

For further information about Stacey and Wesley Campbell and their ministry, please contact:

Stacey and Wesley Campbell
Revival Now Ministries
2041 Harvey Ave.
Kelowna, B.C. Canada
Ph: 888-738-4832
www.revivalnow.com

Endnotes

1. Rom. 8:26 NIV.
2. See Jude 20, and 1 Cor. 14:4-5a.
3. Rom. 12:1 KJV.
4. This short biographical sketch of Brother Lawrence is based on his book *The Practice of the Presence of God* (New Kensington, PA: Whitaker House, 1982).
5. Col. 3:17.

Chapter 6

The Impossible Dream of No Distractions

...when distracted by life's disturbances.

Thetus Tenney

*W*e have all probably had a good case of the "if onlys" at some time in our lives. We are surrounded by a culture of distractions. Just as there will never be a time of "enough time," there will never be a time without distractions. That is the impossible dream. The reality is that the urgent can often crowd out the important. That means we must deal with it by predetermining our priorities and by setting a committed course of action.

You would probably not be reading these words if you did not have a genuine desire to pursue God, and at the same time feel a degree of frustration on how to do this while busily chasing life's challenges. Your spirit keenly feels that pursuing God is your greatest desire and delight, yet your life abounds with distractions. This can produce a big-time case of the "if onlys."

"I would love to pursue God more fervently, if...if only I had more time...if only I had more help...if only others were more thoughtful...if only my family didn't take so much of my time...if only they would do right." The "if only" list is virtually endless, but it almost always includes "if onlys" related to jobs, spouses, children, and the church. If only....

What seems like an unreachable, impossible dream, to pursue God with all our heart, free of distractions and hindrances, will change only with commitment. Commitment to anything means that in spite of—you will do what is right. True commitment is the driving force of life. For our children, this is something better "caught" than taught. Commitment evolves into passion and passion is contagious.

Often, we sabotage our own good intentions of really pursuing God because of a pre-set idea of how it all should be done. Then if we fail to meet the perfection of our mind-set, we abandon the active pursuit. Perfectionism produces procrastination. Procrastination will rob you of commitment. Perfectionism produces Pharisaical self-condemnation, which takes the joy out of the relationship. Joyless duty will also undermine commitment.

I wonder if there have ever been any God-chasers who could not have succumbed to the "I would—if only."

Surely not Abraham; he had his own distractions:

— He had a mandate from God that no one, not even he, understood.

— He had an aging promise and an aged wife, with seemingly little faith.

— He must have been stressed with the responsibility for nephew Lot and his family, whose values and goals differed from his own.

46

— After the birth of his two sons, Ishmael and Isaac, the tension in his family over sibling rivalry erupted into major conflict.

Abraham, many times in his life, could have succumbed to the "if only's." He was a traveling man with a large household, much wealth and much stress, but he had his priorities right— *he pitched his tent and built an altar* in all the moves of his life.[1] Through it all, he was committed to the course in his pursuit of God. He isn't known as the Father of the Faithful without reason.

If you are committed to the chase, somewhere along the way your "if onlys" will become "in spite of."

Jacob, oh Jacob. Had we known him, his twelve boys, Dinah his daughter, and his extended household, we would have labeled them a dysfunctional family. Few parents have suffered a rougher ride with their kids than Jacob. Name almost any problem and Jacob could tell you about it from first-hand experience. He faced family problems, work problems, devastating disappointment and tragic events, but his commitment at any cost kept him in the chase, even if he had to run with a limp. A limp is not necessarily a signature of failure; it can be a badge of success. For Jacob it was a sign that he refused to give up his hold on God during an all-night wrestling match.[2] A limp can mean you just kept going—in spite of the circumstances—you remained committed.

Jacob's passion pushed him to gain the birthright, even though at the time he was probably motivated by material rather than spiritual reasons. In a time of extreme family stress while pursuing family on his way to Uncle Laban's, his pursuit of God intersected with the very door of Heaven.[3] It is surprising how often God is found in the rock hard places of family stress. Coupled with his pursuit of God, the pressures from his mother, his father, his brother, his uncle, his wives, and his children produced a prince with God from a fast-talking, manipulative man. He surely would not have chosen the process but there is no doubt that his pursuit and pressure from family stress "pressed" him into becoming a prince with God.

Bethel, the "house of God," and Peniel, the "face of God," became Jacob's points of course correction in spite of his life stresses. Esau had no limp, but neither did he have direction. Scripture calls him "profane."[4] The root meaning of this word is "permitted to be trodden, accessible." In our language, it means a thoroughfare with easy access. Esau was open to anything or any way.[5] Jacob's passionate pursuit of God gave limited access to much in his life and served as a course corrector to keep him on track. His struggle was worth it. He gave his children the legacy of the God of Abraham, Isaac and Jacob...not Esau.

Even Paul was a survivor of multiple crises and stresses.[6] He stayed on course by the strength of his commitment. He was "...resolved to know nothing...except Jesus Christ and Him crucified." He declared, "...I consider everything a loss compared to the surpassing greatness of knowing Christ Jesus my Lord, for whose sake I have lost all things. I consider them rubbish, that I may gain Christ."[7]

Wistful longing for a preset plan free of the distractions and the "if onlys" will never take you to the finish line in your pursuit of God. It did not for saints before us nor will it for us. Commitment to the priority of your relationship with God will become the stabilizer in your pursuit. It does not come preset or pre-packaged. Constant course corrections will be needed. The Apollo space mission to the moon was only on course one percent of the time. Only by constant course correction was the mission successful.

A statement made by Jesus has at times kept me going when I felt more like a plodder than a racer. With distraction hounding Him and people trying to deter Him from His purpose, He said, "In any case, I must keep going today, and tomorrow, and the next day...."[8] He was steadily moving toward the fulfillment of His purpose, one day at a time. Direction is more important than speed.

Course corrections in the chase are essential. Life changes. Families change. Children's needs change. Your ability to meet the challenges will change. The only constant in life is change. God is the only thing that does not change. So in the midst of constant change, doesn't it make sense to put priority on the one thing that never changes? Your babies need you, your toddlers demand you, your teens practically ignore you, your grown children move on beyond you. Oh, the comfort of the chase after God—"draw nigh to God, and He will draw nigh to you."[9]

There will always be distractions ... and there will always be God. And God will always be bigger than distractions.

Endnotes

1. See Gen. 12:7-8; 13:2-4,18; 22:9.
2. See Gen. 32.
3. See Gen. 27-32.
4. See Heb. 12:16.
5. W.E. Vine, *Vine's Expository Dictionary of New Testament Words* (Old Tappan, NJ: Fleming H. Revell Co., 1981), p. 217.
6. See 2 Cor. 11:23-28.
7. 1 Cor. 2:2; Phil. 3:7-8 NIV, respectively.
8. Lk. 13:33 NIV.
9. Jas. 4:8 KJV.

Beth Alves is an intercessor known by many as the co-founder of Intercessors International. The Tenney family knows her as a faithful praying friend. Her prayers have added blessings to our lives, even when marriage and grandchildren transformed our original family into several families. Beth simply extended her friendship and prayers to include us all. Our entire extended family loves and respects her, and we enjoy Beth's gentle spirit and quick smile.

Tommy and Thetus Tenney

Chapter 7

Making the Menial Meaningful

...when you are locked in the drudgeries of life.

Beth Alves

I grew up with a Lutheran heritage that goes all the way back to the Moravians, so it seemed like I had an innate love of God. My earliest spiritual memory is of talking to Him with childlike faith and *knowing* He answered me. Even though I knew and loved Him, I was a novice at studying His Word. "After all," I reasoned, "I don't know Greek or Hebrew so I can't really study the Bible. Besides, that's the Pastor's *job*." (However, if this was true, then why was the longing inside of me to know and pursue Him never satisfied?)

At the ripe *old age* of 17, I married the most spiritual young man I had ever met (he was 26). On our first night of marriage, he opened the Bible and said, "Beth, we are going to start our marriage out right." Then we read the first chapter of Genesis together and knelt in prayer. This set into motion what both of us so believed, "that Christ would be the head of our home." Yet something was still missing. What was it?

Two and a half years later, our first child was born. I remember holding her above my head in the hospital (after all, God was way up there) and promising God to teach her about Him. To my surprise, within the next three and one half years, I now found myself the mother of three young daughters. Wanting our children to know Jesus with all their hearts, I began chasing God on their behalf with little time to pursue Him for myself.

Every plan and purpose in my life focused on teaching them all that I knew about God. It went deeper than our daily devotions; I made Jesus the center of everything we did. From music to creative "plays" we put on for the neighbors, to teaching them through the Advent Season, which began four Sundays before Christmas and ended on Christmas Day, my purpose was to teach them about the coming of Jesus as a baby. Each year I would plan something *better* than the last. Then there was the Lenten season, which began 40 days before Easter, when I concentrated on teaching them about the power of the cross.

I Became Spiritually Bankrupt

The children consumed my love—and my time. I wanted them to have an intimacy with Jesus, and I tried to parcel out more of God than I had in personal inventory. The sad part was that I was so busy teaching and training *them* that I did not take time with *Him* for myself. I became spiritually bankrupt.

All too soon, they began school. It wasn't long until I became the proverbial "car pool queen." As I sat in the car and waited for the children day after day, I cried out to Jesus, "Please help me! I want to know more about You. *There has to be more than this.* It seems that I have nothing left to give my children."

As always, He heard my prayer and introduced me to the reality of the Holy Spirit. Immediately, the Word of God became alive to me and my prayer life took on a new meaning. I realized that the deeper life wasn't about mastering Greek or Hebrew; it was about knowing Him.

This was exciting and frustrating to me at the same time. Why? Being a busy wife and mother, time did not permit me to do all that my heart desired. When I was reading His Word, I wanted to be praying; when I was praying, I felt guilty because there was so much work to be done.

By that time, we were also taking care of three children whose mother had died, along with two girls whose mother was in a hospital. So we had a total of eight children to care for. In the meantime, the busier I became, the more I cried out to the Lord, "How can I find time to read Your Word?"

No sooner had I cried than He answered me. It came through a speaker I heard at a ladies meeting. She said, "If you take a giant print Bible and read just *ten* pages a day, you will read the Bible through three times in a year." It seemed so simple.

Give Me a Giant Print Bible and Duct Tape!

Before going home that day, I went to a bookstore and bought a giant print Bible in paperback. I went home, divided it into fourths, put duct tape on each part to hold each part together and put the first section in my purse. *From now on,* I thought to myself, *this car pool queen will always have a part of the Bible with me to read and meditate upon while I wait...and wait...and wait!*

Not long after that, the New Testament came out on reel-to-reel audiotape. We purchased a tape recorder and my husband hooked it up to the intercom in our home. Bible tapes played in our home all night! I read the Bible each day as I waited for the children, and listened to the spoken Word each night, so my soul finally began to feel satisfied.

Listening to the Bible being read made such an impact on our lives that when each of our grandchildren were born, we gave them an auto-reverse cassette recorder and a set of Bible tapes. By the time our first grandson was five years old, he had listened to the tapes so much that he could quote several chapters at a time, along with many other key Bible passages!

What about prayer? My prayer time suffered because I had to be "Mom" to so many children, each of whom needed a little extra attention every day. Once again, I cried out to the Lord. This time the sweet Holy Spirit reminded me that there are daily duties that every mother must perform...regardless of circumstances! Then He gave me an idea.

I listed the chores I had to do every day and assigned the name of a child or loved one to a specific chore. We had no dishwasher or clothes dryer at that time, so I decided I would pray for one specific child while I washed dishes. I prayed for another when I sorted clothes and loaded or unloaded the washer. Yet another child became my prayer focus when I hung out clothes each day. I matched the chores with specific people until each person in my life was covered in prayer. Surprisingly enough, the chores were no longer drudgery, and time seemed to fly by!

They All Belong in Your "Pity Pot"

I'll never forget the assignment I reserved for my "commode-cleaning" time slot. That was when I decided to pray for my "enemies" and all of the other things I did not like. One day the Lord spoke to me in the theater of my mind and said, "You brought these to the right place. They all belong in your 'pity pot.'" That was the end of assignments to the commode.

Our three daughters and a fourth whom we adopted are all grown and married to Christian men who serve the Lord. The three children who had lost their mother gained a loving and kind new stepmother. The other two girls went back home after their mother was healed. Over the years, I have been privileged to see the seed we planted in many of those prayers bear a *bumper crop* through our children, our grandchildren, and the other people I prayed for.

I received life as I read the Word of God while waiting for children in the car pool lines, and as I listened to His Word playing in our home each night. The daily prayers offered at my various "altars of worship" each day prepared me for the call on my life today.

After the children were grown, my husband and I attended Bible college and entered a fulfilling life in ministry. Some of my most cherished memories and satisfying times, however, are rooted in the simple yet profound ways God taught me that I could truly "chase" Him while chasing kids. That is true even in the busy lifestyle of today's new generation of parents.

Times change and methods vary, but God will always make a way if you really commit in your heart to pursue Him.

Passion for Him can help turn molehills into mountainous monuments—landmarks that your children will never forget. Take heart...the menial tasks of motherhood can become meaningful to the future.

About Beth Alves

Beth Alves is the president and co-founder of Intercessors International, which has as its primary focus to pray for leaders. She travels and teaches internationally on prayer. Beth has been married for over 40 years to her husband, Floyd. Their life has been blessed and challenged with the wonderful gift of four daughters and fifteen grandchildren.

For further information about Beth Alves and her ministry, please contact:

Rev. Elizabeth (Beth) Alves
Intercessors International
P.O. Box 390
Bulverde, TX 78163

The name James Dobson and family values are almost synonymous. Many people from all over the world have been encouraged, strengthened, and helped by Dr. Dobson in the important arena of family responsibility. We owe him much gratitude for standing firm as a stalwart guardian of families. He has exemplified what he says by his commitment to God, his lovely wife, Shirley, and to his children. We are privileged to count them as friends.

Tommy and Thetus Tenney

Chapter 8

Balancing Responsibilities in the Race

...when priorities and passion are in conflict.

Dr. James Dobson

I can personally identify with parents who feel stretched in opposite directions when it comes to balancing spiritual life and family time. Shirley and I went through a similar era in the first decade of our marriage.

At that time, I believed I was obligated as a young Christian to accept anything asked of me by my church. I served as superintendent of youth, as a member of the church's governing board, as an adult Sunday School teacher, and as someone who was available for whatever special assignments came along. Shirley was heavily involved in church activities too, leading the children's choir and serving as director of women's ministries. I was also finishing a Ph.D. program and carrying very heavy professional responsibilities. It was a breathless time, to be sure. At one point I remember being scheduled seventeen straight nights away from home at a time when we had a little toddler who loved to play with her daddy.

Gradually, I came to understand that the Lord wanted me to use good judgment and common sense in the things I agreed to do—even if they involved very worthwhile causes. There will always be more good things to do than one man or woman can get done. I realized I needed to maintain a healthy balance between Christian duty, work responsibilities, recreation, social obligations, and meaningful family life.

Then I came across two Scripture references that helped clarify this issue. The first is found in Matthew 14:13-14, as follows: "When Jesus heard what had happened [to John the Baptist], he withdrew by boat privately to a solitary place. Hearing of this, the crowds followed him on foot from the towns. When Jesus landed and saw a large crowd, he had compassion on them and healed their sick."

Jesus was undoubtedly grieving at that time over the beheading of His cousin and friend, John the Baptist. He needed to "withdraw privately to a solitary place." Nevertheless, the people learned of His whereabouts and came seeking His healing touch. Even in that painful time of loss, Jesus took compassion on the people and reached out to those in need. From this I concluded that there are times when we, too, must give of ourselves even when it is difficult or inconvenient to do so.

But there was another occasion when thousands of people sought to be healed by Jesus. After spending some time with them, He got in a boat with His disciples and rowed away. Mark 4:36 says, "Leaving the crowd behind, they took [Jesus] along, just as he was, in the boat." Undoubtedly, the large following that day included individuals with cancer, blindness, physical deformities, and every other kind of human misery. Jesus could have stayed there through the night and healed them all, yet He had apparently reached the end of His strength and knew He needed to rest. He and His disciples rowed away, apparently leaving some of the needy people standing on the bank.

A similar event is described in Matthew 14:23, where we read, "And when he had sent the multitudes away, he went up into a mountain apart to pray: and when the evening was come, he was there alone" (KJV).

Just as there is a time to give, there is also a time to be alone, to pray and to escape from the pressures of the day—even though there are worthy things yet to be accomplished. Those who fail to reserve some downtime for rest and renewal—as Jesus did—are risking even the good things they want to accomplish. That is like installing a new sprinkler system in a yard and putting too many outlets on the line. When that occurs, nothing is watered properly.

Let me offer another illustration. Did you know that grape growers not only trim dead branches from their vines but they also eliminate a certain number of the fruit producing branches? They sacrifice a portion of the crop so that the fruit that survives will be better. Likewise, we need to eliminate some of our breathless activities to improve the overall quality of the other things we do.

Having said that, let me offer a word of caution. This need to maintain balance can become an excuse for not carrying our share of responsibility in the church. Pastors tell us that a few of their members do most of the work while most others get a free ride. That is wrong. We shouldn't go from one extreme to the other in our search for common sense.[1]

About Dr. James C. Dobson

James C. Dobson, Ph.D., is founder and president of Focus on the Family, a non-profit organization that produces his internationally syndicated radio programs, heard on more than 3,000 radio facilities in North America and in nine languages in approximately 2,300 facilities in over 93 other countries. His voice is heard by more than 200 million people every day, including a program carried on all state-owned stations in the Republic of China. He is seen on 100 television stations daily in the U.S. He is a licensed psychologist in the state of California and a licensed marriage, family and child counselor in both California and Colorado. He is a clinical member of the American Association for Marriage and Family Therapy and is listed in "Who's Who in Medicine and Healthcare."

Dr. Dobson and his lovely wife, Shirley, have been blessed with a daughter and a son, both now grown.

Endnote

1. From James C. Dobson, *Solid Answers* (Wheaton, IL: Tyndale House Publishers, Inc., 1997), question #467, pp. 493-495. Used by permission.

Chapter 9

The Pace of the Chase: Maintaining Momentum

...when you can't do all that you want to do.

Thetus Tenney

L ife moves in seasons even as nature does, and seasons come and go. Decades have passed on this long and winding road since the season when I nurtured two young children and a husband in traveling ministry. I successfully developed a plan to continue my pursuit of God in that season of my life, but my life now is far different than it was when I was "twenty-something." Seasons of life will often set the pace of the chase, but our passion for the chase must never diminish.

An understanding of the seasons of life can alleviate frustration and guilt and allow you to make decisions from an eternal perspective, decisions that benefit your life and God's Kingdom in the long haul.

As a young mother, I experienced the necessity of spending long hours at home with my children. At that time, we lived in a wooded area with few neighbors. Since my husband, Tom, traveled frequently, I had little involvement outside the home and felt quite tied down. My natural motivation urged me to be up, out, and away; however, my primary responsibilities in the early years of marriage and family determined the seasons of my life.

Alone much of the time with little opportunity for expression and involvement, I battled with resentment and frustration. I resolved the conflict when I decided to fill some of the lonely hours with the kind of reading and study that would benefit me in the future. A studious mind helped a lonely heart.

Before going to bed each night, I set the house in order for the next day. By arising very early in the morning, I gained several hours of privacy for undisturbed prayer and study before my motherly duties demanded my time. I read a wide assortment of books in those morning hours—I even read entire Bible commentaries! In retrospect, that season passed much more quickly than it seemed at the time.

I have now lived full circle. I have few home and family responsibilities now, so I am free to work, travel, and speak. Little did I realize while taking care of my primary responsibility as a young mother, that I was also given an opportunity to develop my future teaching and writing ministry. Those years of study became the foundation for my life's work! Never have I experienced a season for such intense reading, study, and prayer without the simultaneous pressure of producing in various responsibilities of ministry and leadership. Those were tough years, but good years.[1]

Give Them the Greatest Gift of All— A Hunger After God

In retrospect, perhaps this season had more impact on my children than I could have imagined. They were surrounded by study materials in their formative years. They literally woke up in the lingering presence of prayer and overheard many excited conversations of discoveries in the Scriptures as I told my husband about my studies and reading. Maybe I unknowingly gave them one of the greatest of all gifts—a hunger after God, a passion to pursue Him.

My advice to all young mothers with a heart for God is to do what you can now—and don't feel guilty about what you cannot do. Plan and prepare for the future, but do not overload yourself during the formative years of your marriage and children. God understands. Even Biblically, the formative first year of marriage was considered sacred.[2] The priority of national war took second place to nurturing a young marriage. Don't let fruit-producing pressure rob you of the joy of sinking deep roots. It is an important season with important priorities. Tend your "vineyard" well. When another season comes your way, you will be prepared.

During this season of my life, only occasionally could I attend meetings with study groups, participate in lengthy prayer meetings, or enter extended times of personal intercession. Nevertheless, my passion for God prompted me to develop my own plan, to chart my chase at a pace I could handle at that time.

Jacob the God Chaser had his own share of problems and weaknesses, but he has some sound advice for us in our day: "...the children are tender...I will lead on softly, according...as the children be able to endure...."[3]

Committed to Christ, Bound to Family

Children are never a hindrance to our pursuit after God, but they may slow the pace for a season. Marriage, family, and children—these are all God's gifts to us, arranged according to His plan for our blessing, benefit, teaching, and discipline. If you are committed to Christ, you are bound to family. You can resign from a job, a church, a club, or a position; but there is no way to resign from family relationship.[4]

Even if you leave, quit, or divorce—by God's decree you will remain bound to that family mentally and emotionally. The family is God's best training program for character, maturity, and godliness. Every member will have the same courses— loving, sharing, caring, forgiving, joy, tolerance, change, dependence, independence, blessings, needs, and understanding. No one can "skip" the courses, so it is wise to learn from them as they come. Use the season wisely and learn from your mistakes. You will be better prepared for the next season if you do.

"God relate" to your children. In those early years, they have the highest capacity for learning of any time in their lives. Fill these learning years with God and you will receive a double blessing. Establish them on a good foundation for the next season and at this slower pace so you will be able to pause and "smell the roses" along the way.

Springtime in St. Louis usually brought an outing in Forest Park with Tommy and Teri (and as many friends as could crowd into the car). One particular spring we made our pilgrimage to the park when the yellow forsythia were in the peak of bloom. Forsythia in St. Louis causes the landscape to look like it is bursting with miniature suns. It is a spectacle of beauty!

"Look at the Forsythia!"

Throughout the forty-minute drive, I couldn't help but exclaim, "Look at the forsythia, look at the forsythia!" Finally, the teenagers joined in the chorus mimicking me, "Look at the forsythia!" They probably thought they would intimidate me, but there was no way—it was a joyous day for me! I was in the midst of God's glorious creation with my kids, their friends, and the beauty of nature. I enjoyed it to the hilt!

Even to this day, many years later, the sight of a beautiful yellow forsythia bush evokes treasured memories and warm emotions of a day when together we took time out to "smell the roses."

I have always loved and enjoyed nature—everything from sticks and stones to bugs (nice bugs!), plants, rain, and the sun, moon, and stars. What a classroom the world makes! There is an advantage to small steps in the chase! I really can't explain it, but every time I have paused to share a nature moment with a child or grandchild, I experienced a special moment with God.

Before Tommy was two years old, we never went outside at night without him looking for the moon. Gazing heavenward with eyes of wonder he would declare "God made the moon!" Moonless nights brought questions from his curious mind and prompted simple discussions of how God would probably wash the world that night with rain, to clean the leaves on the trees, to give the flowers a drink. Decades later, I still look at the moon and can hear the words of a tiny boy, "God made the moon!" These God moments, shared, probably weren't long strides in the chase, but every step counts.

The Crucifixion and Tender Tears From My Little Girl

I often read to Tommy and Teri, especially at bedtime. Bible stories shared with a young child can be a rich experience, if you slow down enough from doing the next thing, to savor the moment. The story of the Crucifixion always brought tears from our tender Teri girl. I can still recall how touching to my heart were her tender tears in the silence of a contemplative moment.

In my own time of stretching to know God, my mind would have been crowded with the many awesome aspects of the meaning of Jesus' death on the cross, and there is a time for that. But God used my little girl to remind me once again, "...with the *heart* man believeth...."[5] Head knowledge should never surpass heart feeling.

Bible stories weren't all we read together. One of our favorite devotional bedtime books was about God in nature. I have no idea how many times I read and reread the story of the "walking stick"—or the "stick bug" as we (and the author) called it. We learned no great theological truths from this favorite story of the under-six crowd, but I still remember how God provides protection for His creation when I think of the tiny "stick bug" that can hardly be seen on a limb.

Watching a woodpecker on the big pine tree in our backyard gave opportunity to teach my two young children how God provides us with whatever we need to fulfill the purpose for which He made us. Without the "shock absorbers" built into the woodpecker's head, he could never survive the pressure of pecking.

It's Time to Take Your Merry Medicine

Another favorite book of Tommy and Teri when they were a little older was *Miss Pickerel Goes to Mars*. (We read this favorite in the 1960s, just as man was cautiously venturing into space.) It was a hilariously funny little book with absolutely no spiritual truth in it, other than the fact that we all considered it to be a good dose of medicine! (The Book of Proverbs reminds us, "A merry heart doeth good like a medicine...."[6])

With the intensity of all of our personalities, we needed this hefty dose of laughter.

Seeing God things through the eyes of a child will always be enriching. Processing thoughts through the mind of a child can sometimes be, well, "enlightening."

For a period of time before my marriage and the birth of my children, I taught the children of others. In my well-prepared and intense manner, I was teaching a lesson about taking the gospel to others based on the Scripture passage in Isaiah 52:7 (NIV): "How beautiful on the mountains are the feet of those who bring good news...."

Before teaching about the blessings and responsibility of taking the gospel to others, I told the story of Jesus' last time with His disciples on the mount of ascension.[7] With great feeling, I described the receiving of Jesus into the heavens. "As He went up," I said, "what do you think was the last thing the disciples saw?" I got the expected answer, "His feet!" When I told them how His feet had taken the good news to many, a sober looking little girl raised her hand. I paused and she said, "What if He went upside down?" This incident, seen from a child's unique perspective, has furnished me small doses of a merry heart to punctuate my pressure filled life!

Laughter at the Feet of Our Children

Later on, my own children supplied an unending treasure trove of "heart medicine" in the form of unique childlike "wisdom." During supper late one evening, Tommy posed an unusual question to his father (as a result of his avid reading, I am sure):

"Dad, did you fight in the Civil War?"

In shocked amazement, Tom and I both laughed. Teri, who was almost three years younger than Tommy, joined us in hearty laughter and then added her bit of wisdom to the occasion:

"Tommy, Daddy was just a little boy during the Civil War!"

Another time, my husband again received an especially strong dose of "joy medicine" through Tommy. In an attempt to emphasize some good fatherly advice to our adolescent Tommy, Tom finished his mini-lecture with the confident statement, "Son, I've been down that road."

To which Tommy replied, "Dad, it has probably been paved since then."

My five most wonderful grandchildren have also helped me in my pursuit of God.

Shane, our oldest grandchild and only grandson, taught me that the Word really works, even for a child. When he was just a young child, we were discussing fears he had of some new ventures. At my every suggestion he answered, "But what if...." I was getting nowhere with my reasoning, so I went to the Word. I taught him: "I can do everything through Him [Christ] who gives me strength"[8] and "When I am afraid, I will trust in You."[9]

"Shane," I asked, "do you remember our discussion about the universe yesterday—the earth, moon, stars—how big they are and how they hang in space?" (His affirmative answer also included his ideas concerning the space shuttle!) Then I told him, "In the Bible we are told that God spoke, and all things came into being just because He said it. If His Word can make and hold all that, His Word can hold you, too. So when you feel afraid, speak His Word."

Later on, Shane took a trip with his dad and they were caught in a fierce thunderstorm. Shane said, "Are you afraid, Daddy?"

"Maybe—a little bit."

"Mimi [as he calls me] told me some Scriptures so I don't have to be afraid. Let me tell them to you, and then neither of us will be afraid: 'I can do everything through Christ... When I am afraid, I will trust in You.'"

Your Child's Faith May Create a Benchmark in Your Own Faith!

My reasoning only created more doubt and questions in Shane's mind. When I went to God's Word instead, it created overcoming power in my young grandson! I was the one who taught him those Scripture passages, but I really didn't know if they had "taken" or not. Today, the memory of how God's Word really worked in Shane's life has become a benchmark in my own faith in the Word!

Don't be surprised if your own steps in the chase are steadied as you share brief teaching times in the Scriptures with children. Formal teaching times are good and needful, but learn how to slip them into the cracks of everyday life as Jesus did. Don't be afraid to make up your own tune and sing the Scriptures. Take advantage of everyday situations to apply Scriptures.

The teacher will always learn more from the lesson than the student, so there is a double blessing in store when you teach the Scriptures to your children. The very speaking of the Word will bring life and spiritual energy to you for the chase. At the same time, you will be planting seeds of eternal life in the fertile hearts and minds of your children. This will also help ensure that the pursuit of God will continue with your family. This is important because it has always been the will of God that His relationship with humanity be *generational*. Consider three Bible witnesses to the continuing energy and power of the generational race for God—David, Joel, and the apostle Paul:

> *One generation will commend Your works to another; they will tell of Your mighty acts.*[10]

> *Tell it to your children, and let your children tell it to their children, and their children to the next generation.*[11]

> *I have been reminded of your sincere faith, which first lived in your grandmother Lois and in your mother Eunice and, I am persuaded, now lives in you also...*

> *... But as for you, continue in what you have learned and have become convinced of, because you know those from whom you learned it, and how from infancy you have known the holy Scriptures, which are able to make you wise for salvation through faith in Christ Jesus.*[12]

Speaking the Word produces faith.[13] So whether you teach or speak God's Word to a class, a congregation, or into the heart and mind of a single child, you are the better for it.

An important lesson I learned rather reluctantly is that the effect of the Word is not dependent on me or how I feel. What you know and how you feel are often two very different things. Remember that feeling will always *follow* fact—if you don't allow feelings to be the leader. This is why you speak the Word by faith.

On numerous occasions I have risen to speak when my feelings were "slumping in my chair." At times I've felt afraid, discouraged, or worried; but time and again I've discovered that when I "preach to myself," I feel better! My feelings had followed the facts.

Practice What You Preach

The family is probably God's best classroom. As "nearly perfect" as my wonderful husband may be, on occasion he has rubbed my feelings the wrong way! I'm thankful that he has an exceptional sense of humor. It brings a much-needed balance to my intensity! When he notices that I'm in one of my "concerned" moods, he teasingly comments, "You would be unemployed if you couldn't worry!"

When feelings begin to overwhelm me, he sometimes jolts me by saying, "Why don't you practice what you preach?" My husband's wise and jolting comments can be irritating to me at times, but they are true!

Maintain readiness for the race in your home by injecting a perfectly "legal" daily dose of high-powered "spiritual steroids"! Practice using the spoken Word for yourself and your family.

Let me say it again, there is a double blessing waiting when we use the Word. It instructs, encourages, influences, and strengthens everyone who hears it—including you! Post Scriptures on the refrigerator or the bathroom mirror, devise Bible games, share a Scripture at breakfast, or use them in daily conversation and to explain current life situations. Your children probably won't remember nearly all of them, nor, perhaps, will you. However, the Word is a Presence. John tells us under the inspiration of God, "The Word became flesh and made His dwelling among us ...."[14]

During the early years of your family, make sure you pace yourself in your race after God. Remember what Jesus said:

I tell you the truth, unless you change and become like little children, you will never enter the kingdom of heaven. Therefore, whoever humbles himself like this child is the greatest in the kingdom of heaven. And whoever welcomes a little child like this in My name welcomes Me.[15]

You may chase at a slower pace as family duties demand it, but don't think it makes your passion or effectiveness any less! The word *together* is a valued word in the Bible. Jesus said, "For where two or three come together in My name, there am I with them."[16] Who made us think our children could not be our spiritual partners in that supernatural group of two or three believers? The innate simplicity and purity in a child's prayers tend to place the precious commodity of faith at a high level. Never underestimate the prayer and praise power of a child! The prevailing prayers of your child could accelerate the pace in the race.

When my youngest sister, Becky, was about eight or nine years old, my mother became too ill to go to church. Dad decided to leave Becky at home with Mom, and took the rest of the family to church. When we came home after the service, Mom was up and feeling fine. Surprised, we asked what had happened.

"After you had been gone a half an hour or so," Mom explained, "Becky came to my bed and said she wanted to pray for me. She laid her hand on me and prayed. Immediately, I was healed!" In the generation of my grandchildren, my faith still bears the indelible stamp of the worth of the prayers of a child.

> *One generation will commend Your works to another; they will tell of Your mighty acts...* (Psalm 145:4 NIV).

Endnotes

1. Adapted from Thetus Tenney, *Seasons of Life* (Tioga, LA: Focused Light, 1998), pp. 4-6. (You may contact Focused Light at P.O. Box 55, Tioga, LA, 71477.)

2. See Deut. 24:5.

3. See Gen. 33:13-14 KJV.

4. See Mk. 10:7-9.

5. Rom. 10:10 KJV.

6. Prov. 17:22 KJV.

7. See Mk. 16:19-20.

8. Phil. 4:13 NIV, insertion mine.

9. Ps. 56:3 NIV.

10. Ps. 145:4 NIV.

11. Joel 1:3 NIV.

12. 2 Tim. 1:5; 3:14-15 NIV.

13. See Rom. 10:8,9; Mt. 17:20.

14. Jn. 1:14 NIV.

15. Mt. 18:3-5 NIV.

16. Mt. 18:20 NIV.

*"Fearless" and "fervent" easily describe Cindy.
Fearlessness in service and fervency in spirit
distinguish her ministry in many nations. She has
influenced thousands around the world, and
especially the two children who call her Mother.*

Tommy and Thetus Tenney

Chapter 10

I Taught Them How to Walk, Can I Teach Them How to Run?

...when a relay race is better than a solo sprint.

Dr. Cindy Jacobs

The Lord called me to preach the gospel when I was nine years old but didn't actually release me to "go out" until I was thirty. At that time my children were small; Mary was five and Daniel was two.

I struggled accepting the call of God because I wanted to stay at home and be a full-time mom. Now, I realize that not all women will travel as I do, but those who do and have children all have a mother's heart. Their lives are extremely hectic.

People often ask me, "Cindy, your life is so hectic, how do you ever get to spend time with God? When you are home you are spending time with your children, plus you are writing, helping to run an international ministry, and preparing sermons. How do you do it?"

I have learned a number of things while being a God Chaser. Number one is that chasing Him has to remain uppermost in my mind. One day when I was running to keep up with my schedule, the Lord spoke to me and used both of my names. When the Lord uses both of those names together and says, "Cindy Jacobs, I want to talk with you!" I know that I am usually in trouble.

"Cindy Jacobs," the Lord said, "everyone else's name is on your schedule except Mine." I knew what He meant. He wanted my time...He wanted quality time with me.

From that day on, I have tried to schedule Him in my life every day. There are a few days when I am traveling that I can't be as concentrated as I would like to be, but I know that God isn't a legalist.

I also learned when the children were small that I had to live an extremely disciplined life. I couldn't afford to shirk things that others could be slack about, whether it was preserving my prayer time or cleaning my house. One of my life disciplines is to get up and make myself do the things I least want to do each day.

God chasing *along with the kids* was a way that I built time with the Lord each and every day. We read Bible stories together, talked about God, and prayed and sang together. We generally walked and talked with Him each day.

When I was gone, my children would go to bed "listening to Mommy preach"; that way I didn't seem too far away. I had "chased God" to receive inspiration for that message and they were learning right along with me.

We also memorized Scripture together. Before they went down for a nap, we took the time to quote Scripture. It's amazing what they know now that they are grown up!

This concept of "chasing God together with my children" stood them in good stead many times in their lives. One time Daniel had trouble falling asleep because of what I will call "spiritual disturbances" in his room at night. I decided that it was time that he learned his authority in Christ.

I want to interject here that many parents will try and talk their children out of being afraid by telling them that nothing is in their room. Please do not do this. If the children are afraid it is probably for a good reason. Children are very sensitive to the Holy Spirit and to the spirit realm in general. If they are afraid, it is often because they "see" or sense something in the unseen realm. Many parents have desensitized their children to the things of the spirit by telling them to ignore the things that are tormenting them. Rather than ignore them, they should learn to take authority over them.

I taught Daniel to remember and quote Second Timothy 1:7 when he got afraid. It goes like this: "For God has not given us a spirit of fear, but of power and of love and of a sound mind."

One particularly dark night, Mike and I were startled from a sound sleep by the voice of our four-year-old son shouting from the other room. He said, "Satan, I command you to leave my room right now, for God has not given me a spirit of fear, but of power, and love and of a sound mind! You will not make me afraid, but you will leave and go right now!"

Mike rolled over and said to me in a sleepy voice, "Can't you teach him to do that quietly?" We still chuckle over that night. However, we laugh about it with joy, knowing that even a four-year-old who has been taught to chase God will find the authority of Christ in times of need (which comes from abiding in Him) and allow it to roll out of his spirit.

If you feel you have a call to preach the gospel, but you feel frustrated because your children are small, take it from me: These are precious years. What you pour into your children now will pour out of you later as you preach! Even more importantly, it will flow out of your children as well, and in ways that will amaze you.

God leads us all through different seasons of life. The good news is that in God's economy, there is time for everything pertaining to your destiny. I used to be afraid that He would return before I got to preach one time! I really get tickled when I think of that now—I have preached on every inhabited continent more than once.

The season I spent chasing God while I chased my kids was the richest and sweetest time of my life! I see everything that I poured into them in those early years pouring out of them today as they witness, lead people to Christ, and preach the gospel.

Run the race together: It is a relay race!

About Dr. Cindy Jacobs

Dr. Cindy Jacobs is an ordained minister who has often been called a "spiritual warfare specialist." She travels in many nations meeting with leaders and intercessors with a heart to tear down satanic strongholds over their cities, states, and nations. Cindy is president and co-founder of a ministry known as "Generals of Intercession," which is a missionary organization devoted to training in the area of prayer and spiritual warfare. Cindy and her husband, Mike, live in Colorado Springs, Colorado. They have been blessed with a daughter, Mary, who is married to Tom; and with a son, Daniel.

For further information about Dr. Cindy Jacobs and her ministry, please contact:

Mike and Cindy Jacobs
Generals of Intercession
P.O. Box 49788
Colorado Springs, CO 80907
Ph: 719-535-0977
Fax: 719-535-0884
www.generals.org

Some of my favorite scenes as a parent take place at "Paw-Paw and Mimi's" house. (For the uninitiated, that is T.F. and Thetus Tenney—my parents.) It is usually later in the evening. Paw-Paw puts on his bright red pajamas, pops popcorn and the stage is set. One of my children (usually the youngest—but not always) will clamor for a "Goofy" story. This incredibly articulate preacher of over 50 years will launch into a hilariously crazy made-up story about Disney characters, spotlighting Goofy. His stories may have ministered more peace to his grandchildren than all his sermons.

Tommy Tenney

Chapter 11

Stories to Tell Your Children

...when you don't know what to say, tell a story.

T.F. and Thetus Tenney

ne of my greatest concerns for the children of this generation is the growing trend among many churches to disregard and discard the invaluable ministry of Christian education or Sunday school. Those wonderful Bible stories that are so familiar to us must be retold to our children because they become the sure foundation stones for success and godliness later in life.

Without a Biblical Bedrock, They Will Build Their Lives on Sand

One of the great values of Sunday School instruction is that it helps establish the bedrock of biblical values and ethical standards that help adult Christians stand when others around them fall. How many millions of children in Christian homes are entering their critical adolescent years without the Bible foundations that are so crucial to proper character formation? Without this biblical bedrock, we doom them to build their adult lives on foundations of sand that are destined to fail in stormy times.

My husband has preached a sermon he titled, "Stories to Tell Your Children," in which he briefly paints word pictures of great Bible stories that will last a lifetime for children. It is a favorite of mine, and my children will never forget the truth it contains. Why would a preacher "bother" to deal with such a "juvenile" subject? He did it because God chose the subject first:

O my people, hear my teaching; listen to the words of my mouth. I will open my mouth in parables, I will utter hidden things, things from of old—what we have heard and known, what our fathers have told us. We will not hide them from their children; we will tell the next generation the praiseworthy deeds of the Lord, His power, and the wonders He has done. He decreed statutes for Jacob and established the law in Israel, which He commanded our forefathers to teach their children, so the next generation would know them, even the children yet to be born, and they in turn would tell their children. Then they would put their trust in God and would not forget His deeds but would keep His commands.[1]

The writer of Hebrews appreciated the same sort of thing. Think of the stories he retold in chapter 11: Enoch walked with God so long that one day he walked on home with God. What a walk! Noah built a huge boat on dry land, put his family and lots of animals in it just before it rained a flood and the boat floated. Abraham was called to go to an unknown place. He obeyed and went without a map...and what an adventure! [2]

What Does God's Word Do to Young Hearts?

What wonderful stories to tell and retell! The stories in Hebrew 11 are the recounting of the "Spiritual Olympics." They describe how those with the discipline of faith excelled in the race to win the gold despite diverse and difficult situations. What does God's Word do to young hearts when they hear these powerful stories of God's faithfulness...by faith...by faith...by faith?

However, the Bible is not our only source of inspiring stories to strengthen stamina for the race. I have had a few experiences myself, as did my parents and my children. Now my grandchildren hear the stories. How about you and your family?

Early on in our adventures with grandchildren, we discovered that they loved the stories of the "olden" days. It was incredible to them that we were still alive having lived in the days before air conditioning, hair spray, television and automatic washing machines (not to mention dryers!). But woven into all of those "old" stories were timeless testimonies about how the town drunk delivered the "fixin's" for a Sunday dinner after I overheard my parents' discussion and learned that all they had for the family meal was a prayer; and how my dad's prayers became the fuel for our car after we ran out of gas.

One of the favorite stories we have shared with our children and with *their* children involves my oldest sister, Agnes. When she was a little girl, my mother and dad were preaching throughout Texas. Times were tough, and people ate what they had, not necessarily what they wanted.

Agnes, with a child's appetite, came into the kitchen and asked Mother for a bread and jelly sandwich. When Mother explained that she had neither, Agnes left the house. She came back a little later to inform Mother that she had gone outside, climbed up into the old family car, and prayed for bread and jelly.

After an hour or so passed, Mother looked up from her house chores to check on Agnes who was playing nearby. That was when she noticed a little girl coming down the lane with a sack in her arms. Mother asked aloud, "I wonder who that is and what she has?"

Without hesitation, Agnes exclaimed, "That's my bread and jelly!" And it was. The little girl explained, "My mother said that while she was praying, God told her to send you this jar of jelly and a loaf of bread." I think that hearing such uplifting stories of God's faithfulness, especially "angel stories," are a very important part of a child's life.[3]

They Loved the Story of the Gift From a Total Stranger

Our grandchildren also loved to hear the intriguing story of how our daughter, Teri, and her evangelist husband, Steve, received the much-needed funds to finish the trip in their motor home to their next revival. The grandchildren listened in amazement as they learned that a total stranger delivered the money after she knocked on their door while the motor home was parked at a shopping center.

With a grateful heart, I was able to share the story of how my husband, who was two thousand miles away, suddenly awoke and knew in his spirit that his family was in danger. Sitting straight up in bed, he claimed protection for us by the blood and name of Jesus at the very moment a tornado was heading toward our house.

My heart warmed with emotion when I told them about Tommy and Teri, sitting side by side on the edge of a camp meeting tabernacle platform. Exhausted from praying with me, Teri's pretty little face was covered with tender little girl tears as she listened to her brother whisper in her ear. Raising her hands upward, she was baptized with the Holy Spirit. "Out of the mouth of babes...."[4]

Sometimes our children have stories to tell us. Nothing can "put you in your place" better than the pure innocence of a child.

When our Teri was about seven or eight years old, some dear friends made their first recording—a long play record (it was ancient times!). Teri pulled out the record jacket and began reading aloud the information about the artists on the cover of the recording. It described their ministry, their travels, and the various places they had been. Then Teri looked up and said, "Wow, I wish we could do all those things!"

Reconcile the Race From the View of a Child

I was stunned in disbelief. At that time, she had already accompanied us to every location and event described on that album, and many more besides! Reconcile the race of ministry from the view of a child. You are not the glorified sprinter—you are "just Mom and Dad" plodding along. It is a good balance for all of us who are applauded in public to be "downgraded to the common place of home." It keeps your feet anchored solidly for the race.

When Tommy was almost two years old, "Rudolph, the Red-Nosed Reindeer" made his debut on the holiday scene. It was Christmastime and we were back home for a few days. Tom had made plans to be in a little rural church with a dear elderly pastor friend of ours. Tom had agreed to teach the adult Sunday school class just before the morning worship service. The class gathered on one side of the little auditorium, and I was sitting prim and proper giving due attention to my husband with little Tommy beside me on the bench.

Tom made a strong point of the need to stay Christ-centered at Christmas, and added, "Some people seem to be more concerned about a reindeer named Rudolph than about the Christ in the manger!" He earned an instant response from the ever-alert two-year-old beside me! Tommy hit me on the shoulder in excitement and announced very loudly: "Mommy, Mommy, Daddy said Rudolph!" Then he burst into song—"Rudolph the red-nosed reindeer...."

I managed to muffle the next line—"had a very shiny nose"—but the solo had been sung. What could Tom do? He just laughed and said, "He proved my point!" Like it or not, our children are seldom impressed with our public image, so be prepared—take it in stride and keep running.

Blessed for the Future by Remembering the Past

Even now as I write these few simple stories, my eyes are teary, my heart is warmed, and I am blessed for the future by remembering the past. One of the biggest mistakes we can make as parents is to forsake today for the sake of tomorrow. The rich harvests of tomorrow spring up from the precious plantings you make today. As I've mentioned before, never overlook the "mundane" and the "usual." There is gold to be found in every day God gives you.

Since we were involved in the full-time traveling ministry most of our lives, we learned to adapt our family life to the schedules we had to keep. Our summers were spent going from one youth camp, camp meeting or conference to another. We made the best of what many would consider a difficult situation by folding down the back seat of our station wagon to provide ample space for a toy box, picnic basket, and lively youngsters to play and nap.

We transformed many of our lunch breaks into memorable family picnics at a roadside park so there could be running and playing times. This provided exercise for little growing legs, and it yielded a peaceful time for us as parents when a little later, our tired children were rocked to sleep by the motion of tires rolling down the road.

Little prizes pulled from our "surprise sack" every hour or two helped make the long days of travel more an adventure than drudgery. Tom, always the caring father, carefully built in special stops at interesting places along the way, which provided learning experiences and made memories we treasure to this day.

To some, this would seem less than an ideal summer for children. To us, it was the heart of ministry as a family. It also provided the added blessing of bonding our children with a wonderful array of godly people all over the country! To this day, Tommy reminds us of visits to church events equal with national parks. Both included "bonding" time with great men and women of God.

I learned something else along the way as well—it pays to protect and preserve "family" relationships (I'm referring to both your natural and spiritual family). One story about David has always spoken sternly and soberly to me. When a giant threatened to kill David, the mighty (but older) warrior, his life was in great jeopardy. The Scriptures tell us that "the son of his sister, Zeruiah" came to his rescue. In another battle, "the son of David's brother, Shimeah" slew the enemy.[5] Always be careful of your attitude toward the children of your "sisters" and "brothers." One of them could step in and save you from your common enemy some day! Your children may need *your* friends more than you know.

It Was All God's Idea

Marriage, family, and children—it was all God's idea. It is not a burden for endurance, although the process will bring burdens for enrichment. I don't pretend to understand the entire scheme of God. All I know is that when He trains us for the gold, it produces powerful stories about faith and His faithfulness that spurs on the next generation. God had two "kids" in the Garden and the devil got in, but in the end it produced an awesome story of how evil was defeated, and now we are all God-blessed.

Years of ministry have tempered me and raised my tolerance level beyond my idealistic younger years when I couldn't understand why spiritual folks don't always act spiritual. One particular incident at a church conference stands out in my memory. After I witnessed some angry and un-Christ-like behavior between some Christian brothers and sisters, I sought out one of my older mentor pastors for counsel. We went into the little local "café" (that's what they were called before we knew they were restaurants) for a cup of coffee. I described the experience with intense earnestness, and ended with the disturbing question: "How can God put up with this behavior?" I will never forget his wise counsel.

"Thetus," he said, "you have three sisters, don't you?"

"Yes, sir." (This was before my children came along—I was the child).

"Do all of you always act exactly right? Do you ever have a cross word? Do you ever get upset ("Christianese" for *angry!*) with each other?"

"No, sir, we don't always act right. Yes, sir, sometimes we 'fuss.' Yes, sir, sometimes we get 'mad' at each other."

"Do your Mom and Dad still love all of you in spite of your behavior?"

"Yes, sir."

"God keeps loving all of His children too, in spite of our sibling rivalries, bad attitudes, and angry words. Just because families have problems, they don't stop being family."

Point made! Experiencing family, your children, and your desire for their best gives great understanding of the diversity of runners in the pursuit of God.

The race may get rough. Other runners may kick up dust in your eyes or sideswipe you in a push to get ahead, but just keep running. God wants the gold for all of us because we are His children.

Mercy is probably best appreciated when your heart longs for others to display understanding for your child. "Blessed are the merciful...Blessed are the peacemakers, for they shall be called the children of God."[6]

If you are hungry after God but feel the pressure of family responsibilities, then relax, press the "pause" button, and pace the race for the long haul. Learn to see the Kingdom through the eyes of a child.

The prophet said, "...a little child shall lead them."[7] Your children may be trying to lead you.

Listen and join the childish voices crying, "Hosanna! Hosanna!" as they respond in simple joy and praise over the wonderful works of Jesus. It is better than taking a stand on the sidelines with the indignant, critical chief priests simply because you cannot understand how God is working His will![8]

Endnotes

1. Ps. 78:1-7 NIV.

2. See Heb. 11:5-9.

3. Adapted from Thetus Tenney, *Prayer Takes Wings* (Ventura, CA: Renew Books, A Division of Gospel Light, 2000), p. 84.

4. Mt. 21:16 KJV.

5. See 2 Sam. 21:15-17,21-22; 1 Chron. 2:16; 2 Sam. 2:18; 1 Sam. 16:9.

6. Mt. 5:7-9 KJV.

7. Is. 11:6 KJV.

8. See Mt. 21:15.

As a best-selling author, pastor, husband, and father, Dutch Sheets probably best introduces this next chapter:

"When I was offered the privilege of contributing to this book and its all-important theme, it took me all of two seconds to decide that my wife, Ceci, was the most qualified to share with you regarding 'Polishing Diamonds.' I do most of the ministry outside the home; she does far and away most of the ministry inside our home. I do chase both God and kids, but she has the greatest challenge of blending the two. And she does it brilliantly! You'll see why as you enjoy her insights in the following pages."

Dutch Sheets

Chapter 12

Polishing Diamonds

...when you're wiping dirty little faces, you're polishing shiny little facets.

Dutch and Ceci Sheets

On my 40th birthday, my dear, sweet husband, Dutch (for fear of his life), gave me a beautiful new wedding set. Turning 40 was no small thing for me, and he knew I needed help with this "wonderful" milestone. (I tend to grow old against my will!) He came through in a great way. There—in the center of this gorgeous set of rings—was a brilliant marquise-cut diamond.

Shortly afterwards, I was asked to speak to the "Mothers Of Pre-Schoolers" (MOPS) group at our church. As I prepared for the meeting, I felt the Lord prompt me to tell the women to take care of their diamonds. "Their 'diamonds,' Lord?" I asked. "It's a little embarrassing to talk about diamonds to these young moms. Are You sure?"

"Yes," He said. "Talk to them about the precious, colorful, radiant, many-faceted little diamonds in their homes."

The "Facets" of a Diamond Are Called "Little Faces"

I then began to study about diamonds (also known as "a woman's best friend"!), and found something rather interesting. It turns out that the "facets" of a diamond (the precise cuts made in the raw stone to reveal its inner brilliance and color) are referred to as "little faces."

I could hardly believe it: "little faces"? God was giving me a message about children; they are the precious "little faces" in our homes. I couldn't help but think about two beautiful living "diamonds" of my own.

Most people understand that diamonds must be cared for properly. Consider these simple guidelines:

1.   They must be cleaned so their brilliance can be seen.

2.   The settings (the prongs or devices used to hold the diamonds in place on the jewelry) must be checked regularly so the diamonds aren't lost.

3.   Diamonds must never be left in unprotected places.

Much thought must be given to the proper care of precious gems, and the same principles apply to our care of our children—the "precious faces" in our homes.

Dutch and I have been blessed with two beautiful daughters who are 12 and 14 years old at this writing. They are indeed blessings of the Lord, but they are completely different in appearance and personality (one is blonde with blue eyes; the other is brunette with brown eyes). Dr. James Dobson often refers to three types of children: strong-willed, compliant and shy. We have a strong-willed child and a compliant, child. Sometimes it's hard to believe the same two parents can produce such completely different children!

It is tempting to think, *Oh, that Dr. Dobson would give us an easy three-step formula for cutting and polishing the facets—the little character traits—of our children.* God wants us as parents, however, to discover for ourselves the intricacies and untold treasures hidden within our children. This is not an option, it is a command: "Train up a child in the way he should go [and in keeping with his individual gift or bent], and when he is old he will not depart from it."[1] Like mining and cutting diamonds, it isn't easy, either.

Make Sure You Get Your "Diamonds" to Heaven!

Twenty-three years ago, Pastor H.C. Noah dedicated to God the infant daughter of our dear friends and said, "Many people will come across your paths that you will influence. You will affect the lives of many as you minister God's Word to them—but though you can help, you are not responsible to get them to Heaven. This daughter you hold today is the only one whom you are totally responsible for. You are charged with the task of making sure you get her to Heaven." I have never forgotten those words.

It is so easy to get caught up in the hectic lifestyles of our day—we hurry here, rush to this meeting, and fly there. If we are not careful, hardly any time will be left for ourselves, much less for the family. We often have to schedule "family time" on the calendar and then work hard to make sure *nothing* interferes with it.

Due to my husband's busy ministry schedule, we decided long ago that I would stay home with the children and not travel very often. At times, it has not been easy to see my own gifts "sitting on the shelf gathering dust." That was when I had to remind myself that "polishing diamonds" has a much better reward than other more public opportunities. There will be no greater achievement than hearing my Lord say to me, "Well done, Ceci Sheets. You have raised two wonderful daughters who bring Me much pleasure."

While ministering as an at-home mom, I have learned some valuable "diamond polishing" tips that may be very helpful to you:

- *Have family traditions*: Celebrate birthdays as a family; pray with your children at night when you tuck them in; read the Christmas story before opening gifts on Christmas day; take a Sunday afternoon nap together; make cookies together and eat some of the dough; pray together before meals; make their favorite meals on their birthdays.

- *Get to know your children as individuals*. Listen to their dreams...and dream with them! Never discourage their dreams, no matter how grand they are. In fact, encourage them to dream big!

- *Hear the child, not the problem.* Sometimes you can't see the child because his/her problem is screaming so loudly. Look inside the child's soul and be careful to not let the problem dictate the response.

- *Never use phrases like:* "What did you do that for?" "You're stupid!" "I knew you'd do that!" "Shut-up!" or "You'll never amount to anything."

- *Never, ever, discipline your child when you are angry.* You will *not* see the situation in the correct perspective. Have them sit and wait until *you* cool off.

- *Teach them to be responsible for their own actions.*

- *Be ready to say you're sorry.* They learn by watching you.

- *Set godly examples* by what you say, listen to, watch, etc. More is caught than taught.

- *Spend time with God together*: Learn Scriptures, sing songs, pray, and minister to others.

- *Fill their love cup daily*: Praise, praise, praise them.

When my children were toddlers, one of my all-time favorite books was *A Hug and a Kiss and a Kick in the Pants* by Dr. Kay Kuzma. This book helped get me through some of my toughest times.

Dr. Kuzma's book includes a chapter entitled, "Applying the Love Cup Principle." In it, she explains the absolute importance of making sure children receive lots of positive attention daily. We must spend time directly with our children, encouraging and sharing with them words of appreciation. We, as adults, enjoy encouragement. How much more do children!

These "little faces," who are still being polished and shown their value, need to hear accolades from the people that mean the most to them—their parents.

"I Want to Be Just Like You"

The greatest compliment I can receive in life is not, "Mrs. Sheets, that was a wonderful word you shared with us today"; or "You sang that song so beautifully, Mrs. Sheets." My public ministry may touch the lives of thousands, but to me the highest of compliments would be: *"Mommy, when I grow up, I want to be just like you."*

Dr. Billy Graham's daughter, Gigi Graham Tchividjian, gives a wonderful illustration of a day in her life of polishing diamonds:

"Though early morning is not my best time of day, after a couple of cups of coffee, I managed to fix breakfast, wash the dishes, and usher six children out the door to school before heading for the laundry room.

"I stopped abruptly at the door and stood gazing in disbelief at the mountain of dirty clothes. Hadn't I just washed three loads yesterday? Sudden tears of frustration stung my eyes. I quickly brushed them away, a bit ashamed of myself, and put the first load in the washer.

"Then I continued to tidy up, picking up the morning newspaper and various cups and glasses left from snacks the night before. Soon I found myself in my son's bathroom, scrubbing the tub. Once again the

100

tears insisted on imposing themselves against my will. This time they found little resistance. I was frustrated and discouraged, and my self-esteem was about as low as it could get.

"It was still morning, but I was tired—tired of the same mess day after day—of washing clothes that only yesterday I had folded and returned to their proper places; of doing the dishes, only to get them out a short time later to reset the table. I was sick of spending hours cooking a meal that was consumed in minutes.

"Sitting in the middle of the bathroom floor, sponge and cleanser in hand and tears streaming down my cheeks, I found myself fussing, crying and praying all at the same time.

"God in His loving-kindness came to meet me: 'I tell you the truth, whatever you did for one of the least of these brothers of mine, you did for me' (Matthew 25:40).

" 'Lord, even this?' I asked.

" 'Especially this,' he replied. 'Who else is going to do it for me? In all these small ways, you are serving me.'

"Lovingly reassured and encouraged, I dried my tears and continued to scrub the tub."[2]

Remember to polish and guard your diamonds. Think about their value and see their brilliance. Give attention to how they're being cared for and to who is holding them in their hands. You—and *only you*—are responsible for taking your children to Heaven with you. Look deeply into those facets—little faces—and promise them you will *always* be on their side. Give yourself to them, nurture them, help them dream big and give them wings to fly.

Remember that when you are wiping dirty little faces, you are also polishing tiny little facets! Let them shine!

About Dutch and Ceci Sheets

Ceci Sheets is the wife of Dutch Sheets (best-selling author of *Intercessory Prayer*) and the mother of their two beautiful daughters, Sarah and Hannah. She currently serves beside her husband of 23 years as they pastor Springs Harvest Fellowship in Colorado Springs, Colorado. Along with her many roles as a pastor's wife, Ceci also serves as director of the Music Ministry and Women's Ministry in the church.

For further information about Ceci and Dutch Sheets and their ministry, please contact:

Dutch Sheets Ministries
1015 Garden of God Road
Colorado Springs, CO 80907
Ph: 719-548-8226
Fax: 719-548-8793
www.dutchsheets.org

Endnotes

1. Prov. 22:6, *The Amplified Bible.*

2. From Gigi Graham Tchividijian, *Sincerely* (Grand Rapids, MI: Zondervan, 1984), quoted in *The Women's Devotional Bible—NIV* (Grand Rapids, MI: Zondervan, 1990), p. 1245. Used by permission.

Chapter 13

Different Pace—Same Race

...when toddlers turn into teens.

Thetus Tenney

Virtually everyone with children will experience changes in life that accompany the teenage years. I shared some of the changes we experienced in a booklet I wrote, entitled *Seasons of Life*:

"For many years I had enjoyed cooking and entertaining fellow ministers and workers in my home. These times were always special times for the entire family. However, the teen years turned our home into 'grand central station' for my teenagers and their friends. Their plans and my plans frequently conflicted. Tom and I made a decision that during this season it was more important for our home to be open and ready for the younger set than for us to entertain our peers with a lovely dinner.

"Tacos, hamburgers, packing the Colonel's chicken to the park, lots of cookies and gallons of milk became our home entertainment fare replacing beautiful roasted meats with Yorkshire pudding, ham and asparagus rolls, and minted tea. It was a season with memories we still share with a large circle of grown-up young friends. It was a short season. It could never be recaptured.

"I have never regretted one evening that I gave up studying or speaking for an evening to sit on the floor in our basement den with my husband, our children, and their friends involved in a lively discussion with them of whatever the issue of the moment was."[1]

As our lives change with the changing seasons of our family so does the pace of the race. The unquestioning faith of a young child becomes mixed with the "hows" and the "whys" of the teen years as they prepare to chart their own course.

Pace and Position Change for Everyone in the Family

Believe it or not, the parent will also commence to chart a new course. The pace of the chase and the position of the parent changes. Step by step we find ourselves moving a little more to the sidelines of our children's lives and into the position of a coach. The maturing of children necessitates a spiritual maturing in their parents as well. During your children's teen years and on into their adult life, your active involvement in their lives begins to diminish and your capacity for trust is stretched. Perhaps you could say this is the beginning of the long stretch of the race.

Psalm 127:4 portrays children as arrows in the hand of a mighty man. This being so, the teen years must be the beginning of "the stretching of the bow" to thrust the child you have called your own into a winged life. Since you will have less and less control over this life at this stage, then you need more and more solid trust in God.

At this junction in life, I really began to realize that the most important things in my life were not within my total control. That meant that I needed God more desperately than ever. Health, security, the future, my family, and especially my children—they must all be entrusted to Him who is "able to keep that which I have committed unto Him...."[2]

In my simple thinking, trust and faith are "kin," but they are not the same. By faith I declare, "I can!" In trust I confess, "I have." With faith I become aggressive. In trust, I am at peace. In faith, *I take*. In trust, *I hold*. Truly trusting turns my sprints into long, even, steady strides for the chase.

You will experience a new intensity of training to place your absolute trust in God and His Word whenever you watch your maturing child—a part of your very own heart—walk off into life. You will find that the simple "dos and don'ts" of childhood must now be interwoven with "whys and hows" in passionate reasoning from God's perspective.

The times of playing on the floor graduate to lively discussions around the kitchen table or in the den. Where you used to stand at the door to call in your children from times of play, now you stand at the door and release them to drive away—in *your* car. Through it all, I've learned that one "parental position" must never change: the position of bended knee in prevailing intercessory prayer.

Hemmed in by a Squeak

During Tommy and Teri's early maturing years, we lived in a two-level home with a walk-out basement. We had a small den next to Teri's bedroom and just above Tommy's room, which was in the basement. This den was home to a rocker that Tommy still calls the "prayer chair."

It was just an ordinary olive green platform rocker that was long overdue for replacement from long years of faithful service. It had already served us well in the house we had lived in for seven years during our children's elementary school years. Maybe it was the move from Louisiana to St. Louis, or maybe it was the prayer load from the changes in our lives. In any case, the chair somehow developed a very distinctive squeak along the way. I really thought little of the squeak, but it became quite pronounced to our kids.

Tom's habit was always to devote extended time to personal prayer and Scripture reading at night after the family had gone to bed. I had a habit of getting up early for my times of personal prayer, Scripture reading, and meditation—I wanted to get a headstart before the world or the family awakened. (Jesus never seemed to mind having morning coffee with me!)

As a result, our children heard that chair squeak every night and every morning. It seemed insignificant to me at the time, but that squeaky chair made a major impact on our children. I have heard them say, "We went to sleep hearing the squeak of the prayer chair, and we woke up hearing the squeak of the prayer chair."

Hedge in Your Children Through Prayer

In reflection 25 or 30 plus years later, I am reminded of the words of Hosea the prophet: "...I will hedge up thy way with thorns, and make a wall...."[3] Prayer can hedge in our children; it can block their detours away from God. Prayer can go where you can't go, and it can wait for them at a key intersection beyond your knowledge.

Only God knows what blessings and disciplines for our children came from the old prayer chair, and He is the only one who knows how far Tom and I went as we pursued God in that old rocking chair. After two more moves, the well-worn rocker was retired to storage. Even though a fire destroyed the upholstery and charred part of the frame, we just couldn't give it up. Tom and I rescued it, had it repaired and recovered. After placing a small brass plaque of "memory" on the side of the chair, we gave it to Tommy for his 40th birthday. (It sits in his house as an "altar of remembrance," if you will.)

I am constantly amazed with how much my pursuit of my children increases my understanding of my pursuit of God. I am a steward of the will of God for my own life, but the choices I've made (although tentatively at times!) have helped me trust the working of God's will in the lives of my children.

As I struggle to set my course into the divine destiny God set for me, it helps me release my grip on my children as they set the course for their lives. Secretly, I still wish, sometimes, that I could buy a new adult-size playpen for my adult children at Christmas. It may seem silly, but as a mother, I wish I could always protect them from life's hurts. I quickly dismiss my secret wish, however, because I know it would remove them from life's purpose as well as its dangers.

At this point, all of us "worried parents" in the Kingdom are best served by singing together, "Trust and obey, for there's no other way...."

Bond Your Children to Your Peers

As the circle of life begins to broaden with your maturing children, it is important to make sure there are other people in their lives to help guide the way and chart the course. You can safeguard your children and yourself by helping your teens to develop friendships with *your* peers. Every teen needs some trusted adults outside of the home with whom they may discuss ideas, pose questions, and even share confidences at times. To make sure these outside influences share your value system, deliberately bring your teens into the comfortable circle of friendships you enjoy and depend on.

Cross-generational friendships enrich and ensure a safer, better future for the entire family. The Bible says, "Plans fail for lack of counsel, but with many advisers they succeed"[4] and "For lack of guidance a nation falls, but many advisers make victory sure."[5] Counselors can help us all avoid known pitfalls in the race after God, and their wise guidance can help firmly establish a clear purpose for the race.

Both Children "Caught" Our Love for Books

As parents, we should share more than our friends with our children; we should also share ideas, ministry, experiences, and books! These pools of wisdom and accumulated knowledge and experience can strengthen and smooth the strides as you and your children begin to run in tandem the race that is set before you.

Both of our children definitely "caught" our love for books, but not just books, they fell in love with "The Book"...the Bible. Both are ardent students and teachers of God's Word now.

Our children loved their Bibles and read them regularly. Tommy discovered the Book of Revelation during his elementary years and read it over and over. I am sure he was more captivated by the horror, scorpions, and such, than by the prophetic utterances, but there is a blessing pronounced on those who read it that knows no age boundaries.[6]

The prophetic words spoken of Jesus, "...of His kingdom there shall be no end..."[7] speak to me of the ever-broadening scope of His rule and reign. His is an *expanding* kingdom. Generational expansion is part of the legacy of our covenant-keeping God. The unbroken succession of Abraham, Isaac, and Jacob beautifully illustrates this principle of the expanding kingdom. Consider their lives, their possessed territory, their increasing families, and their accumulated experiences and shared understanding. All of it could never have been compacted into the lives of just one generation. Yet God remained the central force from generation to generation.

From Ur of the Chaldeans to the Egypt of the Pharoahs, God remained the one constant unchanged in the midst of virtually constant change. Trust! Understand that "believing" in God must be transformed into solid trust in Him as your children embark on their own personal pursuit of God.

Nothing strikes terror in the heart of a parent like danger for a child. We will go to every length to protect our own from physical harm, but what can we do spiritually?

The Parents Were Commanded to Post the Blood...

The Book of Exodus contains a principle that speaks volumes to a mother's heart. When the death angel was about to be unleashed in Egypt, Moses instructed God's people to put the blood of a sacrificial lamb on the doors to their houses.[8] It was the responsibility of the parents to make sure the children in their homes were safe under the blood. I believe the blood—the shed blood of Jesus Christ, the Lamb of God—still activates protection over homes and families. In our family, we have continuously practiced what we call "pleading the blood" over our children's lives. We do this in our personal prayers, in specific prayers, and in the laying on of hands. At times, we even felt led to prayerfully "post the blood" (represented by anointing oil or simply the touch of a hand) as a symbolic and prophetic act on the doors and windows of our home. Again and again, I've learned to trust God as I cover them in prayer.

The name of Jesus and the blood of Jesus are powerful, but also remember the power of the Word as supernatural energizers of effective prayer. The Psalmist declared, "...Thou hast magnified Thy word above all Thy name...."[9] In my Bible I have marked so many Scriptures of promises concerning children. I have read them over and over for years. At the top of the page I have written the word *children* so I can easily find these favored Scriptures when I need my faith bolstered for my race and theirs.

Do You Pray God's Promises Over Your Children?

Many times I have, and still do, turn through the pages and pray the promises over my children and grandchildren. One of my well-used Scripture prayers for Tommy was found in the Psalms: "But You, O Lord, are a compassionate and gracious God, slow to anger, abounding in love and faithfulness. Turn to me and have mercy on me; grant Your strength to Your servant and save the son of Your maidservant."[10]

For our daughter, Teri, I prayed and watched with wonder that "...our daughters will be like pillars carved to adorn a palace."[11]

Many times I have experienced for my own children what the apostle Paul expressed for his spiritual children in the Epistle to the Galatians, "My dear children, for whom I am again in the pains of childbirth until Christ is formed in you."[12] When we pray the Word and invoke the efficacy of the blood of Jesus over our children, we dispatch powerful protection for them through God-breathed prayers. Let me share a few more Scripture passages that have special meaning to me:

...and all thy children shall be taught of the Lord...[13] [The Lord is coach to my children, and to me.]

In the last days, God says, I will pour out My Spirit on all people. Your sons and daughters will prophesy, your young men will see visions, your old men will dream dreams. Even on My servants, both men and women, I will pour out My Spirit in those days, and they will prophesy.[14]

Your sons will take the place of your fathers; you will make them princes throughout the land. I will perpetuate your memory through all generations...[15]

The promise is for you and your children...[16]

God Is Talking About a Relay Race, Not a Solo Sprint!

Young and old, sons and daughters—it should be obvious that God is really talking about a *relay race*, not just a solo sprint! It is a race where direction is more important than speed, where success is in the running, and the reward comes when your feet touch the gold.

It is a sobering thought to me that the protection of the children of the Israelites was the responsibility of the parents. They, not the children, were instructed to put the blood of sacrifice on the doorway. In doing so, the parents preserved the life of the child. That responsibility is something that does not change although the pace of the race may change dramatically. No matter what stage your children may be in the circle of life at this moment, remember the old song, "Power in the Blood"? It still works for those who trust in it. Above all, remember that the process of "chasing God while chasing kids" was God's idea.

> *Being confident of this, that He who began a good work in you will carry it on to completion until the day of Christ Jesus.*[17]

Endnotes

1. Thetus Tenney, *Seasons of Life* (Tioga, LA: Focused Light, 1998), pp. 6-7. (You may contact Focused Light at P.O. Box 55, Tioga, LA, 71477.)

2. 2 Tim. 1:12 KJV.

3. Hosea 2:6 KJV.

4. Pr. 15:22 NIV.

5. Pr. 11:14 NIV.

6. See Rev. 1:3.

7. Lk. 1:33 KJV.

8. See Ex. 12.

9. Ps. 138:2 KJV.

10. Ps. 86:15-16 NIV.

11. See Ps. 144:12 NIV.

12. Gal. 4:19 NIV.

13. Is. 54:13 KJV.

14. Acts 2:17-18 NIV.

15. Ps. 45:16-17 NIV.

16. Acts 2:39 NIV.

17. Phil. 1:6 NIV.

Dick has committed his life to sharing the gospel with thousands of people around the world. Those of us who know him and his wife, Dee, know that family is a top priority with them. Not only do they fast and pray for the needs of the world's people, but they do the same for their own daughters.

Tommy and Thetus Tenney

Chapter 14

How to Add Fuel to Their Fire

...when it seems like they won't make it.

Dr. Dick Eastman

*I*t was late at night and I was ready to retire after a typically hectic day when the phone rang. It was my good friend Bob (not his real name) calling from the East Coast. Living two time zones to the west, I realized it was even later for Bob.

Bob, a prominent Christian leader and author of several best-selling books, couldn't sleep and wanted someone to talk with. It was about his 16-year-old son who was in deep rebellion and only a few days earlier had left home. Bob believed his son was on drugs and drinking heavily, clearly the result of getting in with the wrong crowd.

"Dick, I don't think I can go on," Bob spoke haltingly, obviously in tears. "I'm seriously considering leaving the ministry," he added with sounds of both doubt and guilt in his voice. I spent considerable time late into the night encouraging Bob, and even relating some of my wife's and my journey years before of praying our two daughters through their turbulent times as troubled teens.

"Don't give up, Bob," I continued, adding, "I'm glad we kept on praying because victory finally came."

A few days passed and the phone rang again late one evening. This time it was another Christian leader, also prominent in ministry, and like Bob, a best-selling author. I couldn't believe my ears when this friend almost parroted the very words of Bob.

"Dick," the voice cracked with emotion, "I just can't get into the pulpit any more with any degree of authority when I realize both my teenagers say they hate me and they hate God. Where did I go wrong?"

Again, I tried to offer encouragement, and, as with Bob, I described some of the prayer journey Dee and I experienced with our daughters years earlier.

Amazingly, over the following several weeks I was to speak personally to three additional leaders, all prominent in ministry (enough so that the average Christian reader would recognize each of their names), all of whom shared similar stories. (Four of the five actually suggested stepping aside from their ministries.) That was five leaders in five weeks, all describing how their kids were locked in some sort of spiritually mortal combat, and four were about to give up! To them, it was a life and death spiritual struggle.

Thankfully, to my knowledge all of these leaders have seen at least some encouraging signs of emerging victory in the several years since I encountered those five rather bizarre weeks. Yet, any spiritually sensitive parent realizes our kids are under sharp spiritual attack, perhaps unlike any time in Church history.

What's a parent to do? How can we chase after God when satan is chasing after our kids—big time? For starters, I believe we need to form a daily "Word-focused" prayer shield around our kids (and grandkids), no matter their ages. We need to literally "pray" our kids into the Kingdom! I am planning a book that will expand on this concept. If we intend to be true "God Chasers" as parents, we ought to determine early on that we intend to "chase" after our kids, daily, through strategic, focused prayer.

I've prepared "A 31-Day Kid Chaser's Prayer Guide for God Chasers" designed to help you do just this. *The Prayer Guide* appears after this chapter (pocket-sized version included inside back cover) and it features a primary "prayer claim" for each day, including a foundational Bible passage as well as a "prayer declaration" that you can speak over your child. I suggest you hold a picture of each child in your hand as you declare these biblically based claims over them. Be sure to read the entire Bible passage as a part of your prayer, and even transform these verses into bold prayers. Then, speak the "prayer declaration" into the heart and spirit of your child. (For very young children you can do this nightly in their rooms while they're asleep.)

A sample prayer (using number one from the following guide) might include:

"Lord, today I claim a spirit and attitude of *reverence* over my son, *Josh*. Your Word says in Proverbs 9:10 (NIV) that 'the fear of the Lord is the beginning of wisdom, and the knowledge of the Holy One is understanding.' I declare over *Josh* a clear understanding of 'the fear of the Lord.' May he deeply respect and reverence You. This day I speak this attitude into his spirit. May *Josh* truly know You, the Holy One, and in the process have wisdom this very day to make right choices. May all of his actions reflect a true understanding of the fear of the Lord. I pray this over *Josh*, in Jesus' Name!"

About Dr. Dick Eastman

Dr. Dick Eastman is international president of Every Home for Christ, a 54-year-old ministry that has planted over 1.9 billion gospel messages home to home in 187 nations resulting in over 26 million follow-up decision cards and responses. He also serves as president of America's National Prayer Committee, and is the author of numerous best-selling books on prayer and evangelism that have sold almost two million copies. As chairman of Mission America's "Light Your Street Network," Dick also helps give leadership to the growing "Lighthouses of Prayer" movement sweeping across America. Dick and his wife, Dee, make their home in Colorado Springs, Colorado. They have two grown daughters, Dena and Ginger.

For further information about Dr. Dick Eastman and his ministry, please contact:

Dr. Dick Eastman
Every Home for Christ
P.O. Box 35950
Colorado Springs, CO 80935-3595
Ph: 719-260-8888
Fax: 719-260-7408
www.ehc.org

A 31-Day Kid Chaser's Prayer Guide for God Chasers

We've provided this Prayer Guide for you in the hope that you will use it daily to blanket your children in prayer. (We have also printed a pocket-sized version of this Prayer Guide and packaged it in the inside back cover of this book. It is designed to be easily removed from the book so you can keep it in your Bible for regular use.)

DAY 1:   Claim a spirit of *REVERENCE*.

Scripture focus: Proverbs 9:10

Prayer declaration: *A respect of the Lord*

DAY 2:   Claim a spirit of *HUMILITY*.

Scripture focus: James 4:7-10

Prayer declaration: *A heart of submission*

DAY 3:   Claim a spirit of *PURITY*.

         Scripture focus: Matthew 5:8

         Prayer declaration: *A longing to be clean*

DAY 4:   Claim a spirit of *PURPOSE*.

         Scripture focus: Proverbs 4:25-27

         Prayer declaration: *A sense of direction*

DAY 5:   Claim a spirit of *SIMPLICITY*.

         Scripture focus: I John 2:15-17

         Prayer declaration: *A lifestyle free of the world*

DAY 6:   Claim a spirit of *COMMITMENT*.

         Scripture focus: Joshua 24:14-15

         Prayer declaration: *A determination to stand firm*

DAY 7:   Claim a spirit of *DILIGENCE*.

         Scripture focus: 2 Peter 1:5

         Prayer declaration: *A willingness to work*

DAY 8:   Claim a spirit of *SERVANTHOOD*.

         Scripture focus: Galatians 6:9-10

         Prayer declaration: *A desire to help others*

DAY 9: Claim a spirit of *CONSISTENCY*.

Scripture focus: James 1:5-8

Prayer declaration: *A lifestyle of steadiness*

DAY 10: Claim a spirit of *ASSURANCE*.

Scripture focus: Hebrews 10:22

Prayer declaration: *A depth of conviction*

DAY 11: Claim a spirit of *AVAILABILITY*.

Scripture focus: Isaiah 6:8

Prayer declaration: *A readiness to obey*

DAY 12: Claim a spirit of *LOYALTY*.

Scripture focus: Ruth 1:16

Prayer declaration: *A zeal for fidelity*

DAY 13: Claim a spirit of *SENSITIVITY*.

Scripture focus: Luke 10:30-37

Prayer declaration: *A heart that is soft*

DAY 14: Claim a spirit of *RELIABILITY*.

Scripture focus: 1 Corinthians 4:2

Prayer declaration: *A depth of dependability*

DAY 15: Claim a spirit of *TENDERNESS*.

> **Scripture focus:** 2 Kings 22:19

> **Prayer declaration:** *A brokenness before God*

DAY 16: Claim a spirit of *MATURITY*.

> **Scripture focus:** Hebrews 5:12-14

> **Prayer declaration:** *A capacity to grow*

DAY 17: Claim a spirit of *HOLINESS*.

> **Scripture focus:** 1 Peter 1:16

> **Prayer declaration:** *A Christlike lifestyle*

DAY 18: Claim a spirit of *COMPASSION*.

> **Scripture focus:** Mark 8:1-2

> **Prayer declaration:** *A capacity to care*

DAY 19: Claim a spirit of *REVELATION*.

> **Scripture focus:** Ephesians 1:15-18

> **Prayer declaration:** *A longing to listen*

DAY 20: Claim a spirit of *SELF-DENIAL*.

> **Scripture focus:** Luke 9:23

> **Prayer declaration:** *A sacrificial heart*

DAY 21: Claim a spirit of *CONFIDENCE*.

       Scripture focus: Philippians 4:13

       Prayer declaration: *A baptism in boldness*

DAY 22: Claim a spirit of *INTEGRITY*.

       Scripture focus: Romans 12:17

       Prayer declaration: *A commitment to honesty*

DAY 23: Claim a spirit of *REPENTANCE*.

       Scripture focus: Luke 3:8

       Prayer declaration: *A willingness to change*

DAY 24: Claim a spirit of *TRUST*.

       Scripture focus: Psalm 125:1

       Prayer declaration: *A reliance on God*

DAY 25: Claim a spirit of *UNITY*.

       Scripture focus: 1 Corinthians 1:10

       Prayer declaration: *A peacemaker's heart*

DAY 26: Claim a spirit of *TEACHABILITY*.

       Scripture focus: Titus 3:2

       Prayer declaration: *A hunger to learn*

DAY 27: Claim a spirit of *PRAYER*.

> **Scripture focus:** Isaiah 40:31
>
> **Prayer declaration:** *A desire to wait*

DAY 28: Claim a spirit of *SUBMISSION*.

> **Scripture focus:** Ephesians 5:21
>
> **Prayer declaration:** *A choosing to yield*

DAY 29: Claim a spirit of *RESTORATION*.

> **Scripture focus:** Isaiah 61:1-2
>
> **Prayer declaration:** *A mantle of reconciliation*

DAY 30: Claim a spirit of *AUTHORITY*.

> Scripture focus: Matthew 16:19
>
> **Prayer declaration:** *A warrior's anointing*

DAY 31: Claim a spirit of *GENEROSITY*.

> **Scripture focus:** Matthew 10:8
>
> **Prayer declaration:** *A desire to give*

GodChasers.network is the ministry of Tommy and Jeannie Tenney. Their heart's desire and ministry mandate is unifying the Body of Christ and pursuing the presence of God—not just in churches, but in cities and communities all over the world.

How to contact us:

By Mail:

GodChasers.network
P.O. Box 3355
Pineville, Louisiana 71361
USA

By Phone:

Voice: 318.44CHASE (318.442.4273)
Fax: 318.442.6884
Orders: 888.433.3355

By Internet:

E-mail: GodChaser@GodChasers.net
Website: www.GodChasers.net

 # Join Today

When you join the **GodChasers.network** we'll send you a free teaching tape and our ministry letter!

If you share in our vision for personal and corporate revival and want to stay current on how the Lord is using GodChasers.network, please add your name to our ministry list. We'd like to keep you updated on the fires of revival being set around the world through Tommy and the GodChasers team! We'll also send schedule updates and make you aware of new resources as they become available.

Run with us by calling or writing to:

Tommy Tenney
GodChasers.network
P.O. Box 3355
Pineville, Louisiana 71361-3355
USA

318-44CHASE (318.442.4273)
or sign up online at www.GodChasers.net/lists/

We regret that we are only able to send regular postal mailings to U.S. residents at this time. If you live outside the U.S. you can still add your postal address to our mailing list—you will automatically begin to receive our mailings as soon as they are available in your area.

E-mail Announcement List

If you'd like to receive information from us via e-mail, just provide an e-mail address when you contact us and let us know that you want to be included on the e-mail announcement list!

Chase God With Us
Daily E-mail Bible Reading Program
An Invitation to Run

If you already have a daily Bible reading plan, we commend you. If you don't we invite you to join with us in reading God's Word. Just go to our website @www.godchasers.net and click on Chase God to sign up and you will start receiving the daily reading! It only takes a few minutes each day to read the Bible in a year. Just find today's date and continue faithfully for the next twelve months.

If you skip a day, don't get discouraged. Don't let minor setbacks become major obstacles. Remember that the goal isn't to follow a "schedule" religiously; the goal is to spend time with God in His Word.

If you find yourself missing days fequently and are tempted to give up altogether, Don't! Disregard the dates and simply read a portion whenever you can. You may not feel like you're making progress, but as you move forward through more and more of the readings, you'll see how far you're really getting and be encouraged to continue.

God Chasers Ministry Internship

I'm excited to announce a brand new GodChasers Internship Program for teenagers and young adults. I want to train the next generation of GodChasers so they can pass on this passion to their friends and communities! This year-long program will include classroom time, practical application and an opportunity to accompany my traveling team on a ministry trip. This isn't a summer camp or vacation—it will be hard work. It will involve a lot of sacrifice. Participants will be challenged and stretched and taken far beyond their comfort zones. It will be an intense, no-nonsense, power-packed time. Real work! Real ministry! Real destiny!

Tony

AUDIOTAPE ALBUMS BY

Tommy Tenney

FANNING THE FLAMES
(audiotape album) $20 plus $4.50 S&H

Tape 1 — The Application of the Blood and the Ark of the Covenant: Most of the churches in America today dwell in an outer-court experience. Jesus made atonement with His own blood, once for all, and the veil in the temple was rent from top to bottom.

Tape 2 — A Tale of Two Cities—Nazareth & Nineveh: What city is more likely to experience revival: Nazareth or Nineveh? You might be surprised....

Tape 3 — The "I" Factor: Examine the difference between *ikabod* and *kabod* ("glory"). The arm of flesh cannot achieve what needs to be done. God doesn't need us; we need Him.

KEYS TO LIVING THE REVIVED LIFE
(audiotape album) $20 plus $4.50 S&H

Tape 1 - Fear Not: To have no fear is to have faith, and that perfect love casts out fear, so we establish the trust of a child in our loving Father.

Tape 2 - Hanging in There: Have you ever been tempted to give up, quit, and throw in the towel? This message is a word of encouragement for you.

Tape 3 - Fire of God: Fire purges the sewer of our souls and destroys the hidden things that would cause disease. Learn the way out of a repetitive cycle of seasonal times of failure.

NEW!
WHAT'S THE FIGHT ABOUT?
(audiotape album) $20 plus $4.50 S&H

Tape 1 - Preserving the Family: God's special gift to the world is the family. If we don't preserve the family, the Church is one generation from extinction. God's desire is to heal the wounds of the family from the inside out.

Tape 2 - Unity in the Body: An examination of the levels of Unity that must be respected and achieved before "Father, let them be one" becomes an answered prayer!

Tape 3 - What's the Fight About?: If you're throwing dirt, you're just loosing ground! In **What's the Fight About?** Tommy invades our backyards to help us discover our differences aren't so different after all!

TURNING ON THE LIGHT OF THE GLORY
(video) $20 plus $4.50 S&H

Tommy deals with turning on the light of the glory and presence of God, and he walks us through the necessary process and ingredients to potentially unleash what His Body has always dreamed of.

THREE NEW VIDEOS BY

LET'S BUILD A BONFIRE VOL. 1:
LET IT FALL
(video) $20 plus $4.50 S&H

One hour of the best worship and word
from the GodChaser gatherings.

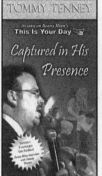

CAPTURED IN
HIS PRESENCE
(1 hour video)
$25 plus $4.50 S&H

An encounter with God captured on tape as
seen on *This Is Your Day* with Benny Hinn.

FOLLOW THE MAN
ON THE COLT
(1 hour video) $20 plus $4.50 S&H

Are you too proud to ride with Him? Humility
is the catalyst that will move your answers
from a crawl to a walk to a run and to a ride.

Tommy Tenney has touched the heart of a generation who crave for an encounter with their Lord.
The passion of his heart, captured in his writings, has
ignited a flame of godly pursuit across this world.

The Daily Chase offers you the best of those writings. Each day there awaits you a fresh encounter with
the One you long for. Don't hold anything back.

Sample God Chaser Worship CD' enclosed in back of
book includes:

• Sample songs from Jeannie Tenney's album "Holy Hunger"

• Sample songs from a NEW God Chaser worship album

• Sample video clips from the accompanying music video

*1st printing only

Elegant Case Bound Edition, $19.00

Run With Us!

Become a GodChasers Monthly Revival Partner

Two men, a farmer and his friend, were looking out over the farmer's fields one afternoon. It was a beautiful sight—it was nearly harvest time, and the wheat was swaying gently in the wind. Inspired by this idyllic scene, the friend said, "Look at God's provision!" The farmer replied, "You should have seen it when God had it by Himself!"

This humorous story illustrates a serious truth. Every good and perfect gift comes from Him: but we are supposed to be more than just passive recipients of His grace and blessings. We must never forget that only God can cause a plant to grow—*but it is equally important to remember that we are called to do our part in the sowing, watering, and harvesting.*

When you sow seed into this ministry, you help us reach people and places you could never imagine. The faithful support of individuals like you allows us to send resources, free of charge, to many who would otherwise be unable to obtain them. Your gifts help us carry the Gospel all over the world—including countries that have been closed to evangelism. Would you prayerfully consider becoming a revival partner with us? As a small token of our gratitude, our Revival Partners who send a monthly gift of $20 or more receive a teaching tape and ministry letter every month. This ministry could not survive without the faithful support of partners like you!

Stand with me now—so we can run together later!

In Hot Pursuit,

Tommy Tenney

Tommy Tenney
& The GodChasers.network Staff

Become a Monthly Revival Partner by calling or writing to:

Tommy Tenney/GodChasers.network

P.O. Box 3355
Pineville, Louisiana 71361-3355
318.44CHASE (318.442.4273)

Other books by Thetus Tenney

PRAYER TAKES WINGS

This insightful work discusses and documents the interaction of angels with our prayers. Follow through the Scriptures and these pages as the relationship between prayer and the directed intervention of angels in our worldly existence is revealed.

"...FIRST OF ALL..." PRAYER

An excellent resource manual from the author and her daughter, Teri Spears. Here are creative ways to enrich your personal and corporate prayer life, lead prayer meetings, pray for your family and your world, set up prayer rooms, study and teach the Scriptures, and influence your community. Comes in a user-friendly loose-leaf notebook format.

FOCUSED LIGHT, VOL. 1

Concise but very powerful Bible studies on prayer, praise, faith and spiritual warfare. This is an excellent resource for personal spiritual growth or for use with small or large groups.

FOCUSED LIGHT, VOL. 2

Sequel study to Volume 1 on prayer, praise, faith, and spiritual warfare.

SEASONS OF LIFE

This booklet is a condensed version of one of Thetus Tenney's most requested messages. In it, she share thoughts concerning women in all stages of life.

Focused Light
P.O. Box 55
Tioga, LA 71477
Phone: 1-888-433-3355
E-mail: ThetusTenney@aol.com

Exciting titles
by Tommy Tenney

► GOD'S FAVORITE HOUSE

The burning desire of your heart can be fulfilled. God is looking for people just like you. He is a Lover in search of a people who will love Him in return. He is far more interested in you than He is interested in a building. He would hush all of Heaven's hosts to listen to your voice raised in heartfelt love songs to Him. This book will show you how to build a house of worship within, fulfilling your heart's desire and His!
ISBN 0-7684-2043-1

► THE GOD CHASERS (Best-selling **Destiny Image** book)

There are those so hungry, so desperate for His presence, that they become consumed with finding Him. Their longing for Him moves them to do what they would otherwise never do: Chase God. But what does it really mean to chase God? Can He be "caught"? Is there an end to the thirsting of man's soul for Him? Meet Tommy Tenney—God chaser. Join him in his search for God. Follow him as he ignores the maze of religious tradition and finds himself, not chasing God, but to his utter amazement, caught by the One he had chased.
ISBN 0-7684-2016-4
Also available in Spanish
ISBN 0-7899-0642-2

► GOD CHASERS DAILY MEDITATION & PERSONAL JOURNAL

Does your heart yearn to have an intimate relationship with your Lord? Perhaps you long to draw closer to your heavenly Father, but you don't know how or where to start. This *Daily Meditation & Personal Journal* will help you begin a journey that will change your life. As you read and journal, you'll find your spirit running to meet Him with a desire and fervor you've never before experienced. Let your heart hunger propel you into the chase of your life…after God!
ISBN 0-7684-2040-7

► SECRET SOURCES OF POWER

by T.F. Tenney with Tommy Tenney.
Everyone is searching for power. People are longing for some external force to empower their lives and transform their circumstances. *Secret Sources of Power* furnishes some of the keys that will unlock the door to Divine power. You might be surprised at what is on the other side of that door. It will be the opposite of the world's concepts of power and how to obtain it. You will discover that before you lay hold of God's power you must let go of your own resources. You will be challenged to go down before you can be lifted up. Death always comes before resurrection. If you are dissatisfied with your life and long for the power of God to be manifested in you then now is the time. Take the keys and open the door to *Secret Sources of Power*!
ISBN 0-7684-5000-4

Available at your local Christian bookstore.